Claude Anctil
Sept. 17, 1963

READING THE WORD OF GOD

Lawrence Dannemiller, S. S.

1960
Helicon Press
Baltimore

Nihil obstat: EDWARD A. CERNY, S.S., S.T.D.
Censor Librorum

Imprimatur: † FRANCIS P. KEOUGH, D.D.
Archbishop of Baltimore
January 4, 1960

The *Nihil obstat* and *Imprimatur* are official declarations that a book or pamphlet is free of doctrinal or moral error. No implication is contained therein that those who have granted the *Nihil obstat* and *Imprimatur* agree with the opinions expressed.

Second Printing, November 1962

Library of Congress Catalog Card Number: 60–9792

First published by Helicon Press, Inc., Baltimore 27.

PRINTED IN THE UNITED STATES OF AMERICA BY THE NORTH CENTRAL PUBLISHING COMPANY, ST. PAUL, MINNESOTA.

PREFACE

ESSENTIALLY THIS work is meant to bring its users to the Scriptures, "which are able to instruct you unto salvation by the faith which is in Christ Jesus" and "that the man of God may be perfect, equipped for every good work" (2 Tm. 3, 15–17). There are today many outstanding books which contain an abundance of information about the Bible; they have played, and do play, an important part in the present-day renewal of interest in the Bible. But few of these excellent books can be said to lead the reader directly to the sacred text.

It is very important that the reading of the Bible not take second place to reading about the Bible or to any other form of reading, no matter how edifying. For the Christian, the Bible is the first of all books, it is The Book. The Church reads the Bible every day as did the synagogue from which she learned the practice. The Fore-Mass or Mass of the Catechumens as well as the Divine Office are basically services devoted to reading the Word of God. The Bible is our chief source of theology; its spirituality, if we make it our own, will bring us ever closer to the mind and heart of the Church. It is not just a book for scholars to ponder; it is the Word of God and should pervade our daily spiritual lives, our teaching and preaching, if ever we are to attain to a rightful understanding and love for Christ. In the words of St. Jerome, "To be ignorant of the Scriptures is to be ignorant of Christ."

It is true that reading the Bible can present difficulties. How many of us who acknowledge the importance of reading the Bible have begun with great resolution at the beginning only to have the resolution dwindle in the face of obscure passages or long statistics? To avoid these problems, some guides to Bible-reading furnish an introduction to each of the 72 books and suggest suitable readings therefrom. There is much to be said for this method. However, it can very well happen that a reader using this method will progress book-by-book from Genesis to the Apocalypse and in the end be not very sure what the Bible "is about."

The various events narrated in the Bible are not isolated one from the other; they are not unrelated. The Bible has a plan; it is called "salvation history." So that the reader can perceive the threads of this history, each unit in this book is made up of readings on a particular theme. Sometimes the theme is from one book of the Bible; more often it is drawn from three or four books, as for example in unit 53 where Christ is foreshadowed by the lamb in Exodus, is described as the Lamb of God in John, and is the victorious Lamb of the Apocalypse. In this way, the reader will be able to compare the readings and meditate upon their relationship. It is the Spirit of God, the principal author of the written Word, who speaks in each of the readings; for that reason there is a harmony throughout the whole of revelation, expressed by St. Augustine: "Novum in Vetere latet; Vetus in Novo patet (The New is hidden in the Old; the Old is manifest in the New)."

This comparison or confrontation of texts is not a new idea. In the Missal, texts from all parts of the Scriptures are juxtaposed. The practice was common in Old Testament times. The People of God have always tried to understand the present and future in the light of God's deeds of the past.

A few words about the physical arrangement of this book will facilitate its use.

The first part of the text, the "Salvation History," is designed to correlate the entire series of readings into a meaningful whole. It is suggested that the reader return to this section every three or four months if the reading is done weekly, or at equivalent intervals according to the rate of reading.

The main body of readings is arranged in 150 units which are supplemented by 75 more units in Appendix A. Each unit is, of course, a whole. The individual unit is arranged for group reading, with a liturgy-like format, employing a leader, readers, and the "congregation." Suggestions for group reading are given in Appendix C.

Each unit is made up of an introductory paragraph, three to four readings, and a concluding prayer. Following the introductory paragraph there is an introductory Psalm which sets the scene for the reading or suggests the sentiments that should fill those who are about to read the Word of God. Following each reading there is a Psalm that is related to that particular reading, and this response attempts to interpret or relate the reading for the reader.

From the foregoing, a reader might gain the impression that this book is meant to be as flexible as possible. It is. And especially in two respects: make-up and use.

Bible reading may be done using the sequence of readings in the main body of the text; this order is roughly chronological. Or, the order of the readings as they are mentioned in the Salvation History may be followed, for every unit in the body of the text and in Appendix A is covered in the section dealing with Salvation History. The readings may also be made according to the Liturgical Year (See Appendix B).

The juxtaposition of texts within the units is not arbitrary, although in some cases a certain accommodation of the strict meaning of a passage has been necessary. The reader should, however, remind himself occasionally that this is not a scientific book and because a text has been referred to a given doctrine, say that of the sacrament of penance, he must not infer that the text proves the doctrine.

Again, a leader of a group or an individual may feel that a text other than the one called for in our arrangement would be more appropriate; he is encouraged to make substitutions.

Especially in the responses substitutions may be necessary. In many cases, passages from Sirach, Proverbs, and so on, are called for in our units. A particular group using this book may find that it is not feasible for all members of the group to have a Bible and the leader may decide that they should use a Psalter.

The public reading of a unit takes approximately fifteen minutes. Each unit could, therefore, serve effectively as the opening or closing of meetings of fraternities, sodalities, and so on.

The book may be used in catechetics, from about the fifth grade on. Since the units are thematic, the teacher will find that they are easily keyed to the various textbooks.

Bible study clubs, too, may find the arrangement of texts useful and less discouraging than the book-by-book approach. As a matter of fact, it would not be presumptuous to suggest that courses in biblical theology be supplemented by this book on the college and seminary level.

It is the hope of the author that the book will be useful as a guide to mental prayer based on the text of Sacred Scripture. Few make mental prayer on the Bible, probably because the text of Sacred Scripture is not systematic. The format of each unit of this book can provide a method of mental prayer on the Scriptures.

The author wishes to express his sincere thanks to the Very Reverend Lloyd P. McDonald, Provincial of the Sulpicians of the United States, for his kind permission to publish this book. Also for their valuable suggestions he would like to thank the Rev. Raymond E. Brown, S.S., of St. Mary's Seminary, Baltimore; the Rev. Joseph Connolly of St. Gregory's Church, Baltimore; and Mr. Lawrence Brett, a seminarian studying for the diocese of Bridgeport. He is indebted also to the students of St. Mary's Seminary, Baltimore, for their searching the Scriptures, typing and proofreading. Finally he would like to add a note of dedication of this, his first book, to his beloved parents who have always been for him a living model of Christian example, parental kindness and generosity.

For the New Testament the Scripture references are from the Confraternity translation. For the Old Testament they are from the Confraternity for Genesis to Ruth and Job to Sirach (Ecclesiasticus); the rest of the Old Testament is from the Challoner-Douay text. Readers using other translations should not find too much trouble in finding the exact versification, although there may be a one or two verse variation.

LAWRENCE DANNEMILLER, S.S.

TABLE OF CONTENTS

Preface iii
The Order of the Books of the Bible xi
The System of Abbreviation Used in this Book xiii
PART ONE: Salvation History 1
PART TWO: Scripture Readings 19

Reading	*Page*
1. Creation in Genesis	21
2. Creation and the Fall of Man	22
3. Redemption	23
4. The Call of the Chosen People	24
5. Abraham	25
6. Joseph	26
7. Israel's Deliverance from Egypt	27
8. The Israelites at Mount Sinai	28
9. The Presence of God in the Cloud	29
10. Aaron	30
11. From the Book of Leviticus	31
12. The Feast of Atonement	32
13. The Feast of Tabernacles	33
14. The Feast of Passover	35
15. The Feast of Pentecost	36
16. From the Book of Numbers	37
17. From the Book of Deuteronomy	38
18. From the Book of Josue	39
19. From the Book of Judges	40
20. Ruth	41
21. Samuel, Prophet of God	42
22. Saul, First King of Israel	43
23. David	44
24. Solomon	45
25. Elias	47
26. Eliseus	48
27. Isaias	49
28. Jeremias	50
29. The Fall of Jerusalem (587 B.C.)	51
30. Ezechiel	52
31. The Return from Exile	53
32. Esdras	54
33. Nehemias	55
34. From the First Book of Machabees	57
35. From the Second Book of Machabees	58
36. From the Book of Daniel	59
37. The New Covenant	60
38. The New Covenant	61
39. Christ, Virgin-Born	62
40. The Epiphany of Jesus	63
41. The Good News	64
42. St. John the Baptist	65
43. The Baptism of Jesus	66

Reading *Page*
44. The Temptations of Jesus 68
45. The Twelve Apostles 69
46. Christ the Divine Physician 70
47. Christ's Power over Leprosy 71
48. The Power of Christ over the Sea 72
49. Christ Transfigured 73
50. Christ, the New Adam 74
51. Christ, the New Moses 75
52. Christ, the Incarnate Word of God 76
53. Christ, the Lamb of God 78
54. Christ, the Temple of God 79
55. Christ, the Light of the World 80
56. Jesus Christ, Life-Giver 81
57. Christ the Rock 82
58. The Good Shepherd 83
59. Christ the King 84
60. Christ the Prophet 85
61. Jesus, as the Lord 86
62. Jesus, as the Son of God 87
63. The Name "Jesus" 88
64. Jesus' Name "Christ" 90
65. Jesus Christ, Son of David 91
66. Christ, the Prince of Peace 92
67. The Wisdom of Christ 93
68. The Mercy of Christ 94
69. Christ's Love for Sinners 95
70. The Charity of Christ 96
71. The Justice of Christ 97
72. The Patience of Christ 98
73. The Suffering Messias 99
74. Jesus Lifted Up on the Cross 100
75. The Resurrection of Christ 102
76. Three Appearances of Jesus After the Resurrection 103
77. The Ascension of Jesus into Heaven 104
78. Anointing by the Spirit of God 105
79. The Church as One 106
80. The Church as Holy 107
81. The Church as Catholic 108
82. The Church as Apostolic 110
83. The Church Composed of the Poor and Humble 111
84. The Church as the New Jerusalem 112

Reading *Page*
85. The Church as the Mystical Body of Christ 113
86. The Church, the Ark of Salvation 114
87. The Church as the Bride of Christ 115
88. The Church as the New Kingdom 116
89. The Church as a Vineyard 117
90. The Church, the Temple of God 118
91. Baptism 119
92. Baptism 121
93. Confirmation 122
94. Confirmation 123
95. The Holy Eucharist 124
96. The Holy Eucharist 125
97. The Sacrament of Penance 126
98. The Sacrament of Penance 127
99. Extreme Unction 128
100. Extreme Unction 129
101. The Priesthood 130
102. The Priesthood 132
103. Matrimony 133
104. Matrimony 134
105. Mary, the Daughter of Sion 135
106. Mary as Mother 136
107. Mary, Ark of the Covenant 137
108. Mary, the New Eve 138
109. St. Peter 140
110. The Primacy of Peter 141
111. St. Peter's Preaching 142
112. St. Paul 143
113. St. John, Son of Zebedee 144
114. Martyrs 145
115. Confessors 146
116. Virgins 147
117. Holy Women in the Bible 149
118. The Following of Christ 150
119. Hearing the Word of God 151
120. Prayer 152
121. Prayer in Common 153
122. Fasting 154
123. Good Example 155
124. Work 156
125. Faith 157
126. Hope 158
127. Charity: the Love of God 159

Reading	*Page*
128. Charity: the Love of Neighbor	160
129. Humility	161
130. Poverty	163
131. The First Commandment	164
132. The Second Commandment	165
133. The Third Commandment	166
134. The Fourth Commandment	167
135. The Fifth Commandment	168
136. The Sixth and Ninth Commandments	169
137. The Seventh and Tenth Commandments	171
138. The Eighth Commandment	172
139. Sin	173
140. Pride	174
141. Envy	175
142. Sloth	176
143. An Evil and Lying Tongue	177
144. Death	178
145. The Resurrection of the Just	180
146. The Judgment of the Last Day	181
147. Christ Our Judge	182
148. Heaven	183
149. Hell	184
150. Christ in His Glory	185

APPENDIX A: Additional Bible Readings 187
APPENDIX B: Suggested Readings for the Liturgical Year 191
APPENDIX C: Suggestions for Group-Use of this Book 194
APPENDIX D: Conclusions for Final Prayers 197
INDEX 199

THE ORDER OF THE BOOKS OF THE BIBLE

For those who may be using a Bible which follows the Hebrew tradition (non-Catholic Bibles) for numbering the Psalms, there is this difference from the Greek tradition (Catholic Bible):

Catholic	*Non-Catholic*
Pss. 1–8	Pss. 1–8
9a–9b	9–10
10–112	11–113
113a–113b	114–115
114 –115	116a–116b
116 –145	117 –146
146 –147	147a–147b
148 –150	148 –150

In general the numbers of the Psalms in the non-Catholic are one ahead of those in the Catholic Bible.

OLD TESTAMENT

Genesis
Exodus
Leviticus
Numbers
Deuteronomy
Josue
Judges
Ruth
First Samuel (First Kings)
Second Samuel (Second Kings)
Third Kings
Fourth Kings
First Chronicles (First Paralipomenon)
Second Chronicles (Second Paralipomenon)
Esdras (First Esdras)
Nehemias (Second Esdras)
Tobias
Judith
Esther
Job

Psalms
Proverbs
Ecclesiastes
Canticle of Canticles
Wisdom
Sirach (Ecclesiasticus)
Isaias
Jeremias
Lamentations
Baruch
Ezechiel
Daniel
Osee
Joel
Amos
Abdias
Jonas
Micheas
Nahum
Habacuc
Sophonias
Aggeus
Zacharias
Malachias
First Machabees
Second Machabees

NEW TESTAMENT

Gospel according to St. Matthew
Gospel according to St. Mark
Gospel according to St. Luke
Gospel according to St. John
Acts of the Apostles
Epistle to the Romans
First Corinthians
Second Corinthians
Galatians
Ephesians
Philippians
Colossians
First Thessalonians
Second Thessalonians
First Timothy
Second Timothy
Titus
Philemon
Hebrews
Epistle of St. James
First Epistle of St. Peter
Second Epistle of St. Peter
First Epistle of St. John
Second Epistle of St. John
Third Epistle of St. John
Epistle of St. Jude
Apocalypse

THE SYSTEM OF ABBREVIATION USED IN THIS BOOK

Abd.	Abdias
Acts	Acts of the Apostles
Ag.	Aggeus
Am.	Amos
Ap.	Apocalypse
Bar.	Baruch
1 Chron.	First Chronicles
2 Chron.	Second Chronicles
Col.	Colossians
1 Cor.	First Corinthians
2 Cor.	Second Corinthians
Ct.	Canticle of Canticles
Dn.	Daniel
Dt.	Deuteronomy
Eccl.	Ecclesiastes
Eph.	Ephesians
Esd.	Esdras
Est.	Esther
Ex.	Exodus
Ez.	Ezechiel
Gal.	Galatians
Gn.	Genesis
Hb.	Habacuc
Heb.	Hebrews
Is.	Isaias
Jas.	Epistle of St. James
Jb.	Job
Jdt.	Judith
Jer.	Jeremias
Jgs.	Judges
Jl.	Joel
Jn.	Gospel according to St. John
1 Jn.	First Epistle of St. John
2 Jn.	Second Epistle of St. John
3 Jn.	Third Epistle of St. John
Jon.	Jonas
Jos.	Josue
Jud.	Epistle of St. Jude
1 Kgs.	First Kings
2 Kgs.	Second Kings
3 Kgs.	Third Kings
4 Kgs.	Fourth Kings
Lam.	Lamentations
Lk.	Gospel according to St. Luke
Lv.	Leviticus
Mal.	Malachias
1 Mc.	First Machabees
2 Mc.	Second Machabees
Mi.	Micheas
Mk.	Gospel according to St. Mark
Mt.	Gospel according to St. Matthew
Na.	Nahum
Neh.	Nehemias
Nm.	Numbers
Os.	Osee
1 Par.	First Paralipomenon
2 Par.	Second Paralipomenon
Phil.	Philippians

Phlm.	Philemon
Prv.	Proverbs
Ps(s).	Psalm(s)
1 Pt.	First Epistle of St. Peter
2 Pt.	Second Epistle of St. Peter
Rom.	Epistle to the Romans
Ru.	Ruth
Sir.	Sirach
1 Sm.	First Samuel
2 Sm.	Second Samuel
So.	Sophonias
Tb.	Tobias
1 Thes.	First Thessalonians
2 Thes.	Second Thessalonians
Ti.	Titus
1 Tm.	First Timothy
2 Tm.	Second Timothy
Wis.	Wisdom
Za.	Zacharias

PART ONE: SALVATION HISTORY

THE BIBLE is the story of man's salvation, prepared for in the Old Testament and accomplished in the New. The central figure in this great drama is Jesus Christ. God constantly visits man by His grace, but man repeatedly resists by his sin. The Saviour comes, fulfilling the hope of centuries, but He is rejected by Israel, His People. "He came unto His own, and His own received Him not. But to as many as received Him He gave the power of becoming sons of God . . ." (Jn. 1, 11–12), members of His kingdom, the Church. The story of salvation, begun with Adam, and fulfilled in Jesus Christ, continues to our own day in the Church, the Mystical Body of Christ. Christ lives on in His members, who await His final coming on the Last Day, when He shall judge the living and the dead.

The story of the religious history of mankind is called Salvation History, to be carefully distinguished from history in the modern sense. Salvation History is indeed a kind of history, for it deals with real events, but it is not history for history's sake — it is not scientific history. This distinction between Salvation History and scientific history must be stressed if we are ever going to be able to pray the Bible. If we want to study the scientific history of Israel we can go to historians like Albright or Noth. If we want to study Salvation History, there is one book alone which contains it, the Bible.

An acquaintance with this religious history of mankind is essential to an understanding of the Christian faith. Man can only understand what God does for him in the present and what He will do for him in the future by studying what God has done for him in the past. He discovers his way to God by retracing the steps by which God came to him, and these steps are the contents of Salvation History. This has been the Judeo-Christian method of prayer, vocal and oral, for three thousand years.

It was the prayer of the Old-Testament man to ponder the *magnalia Dei* — to recall past favors of God, relate them to the present, and hope in terms of these favors for the future. That is what Mary, the Mother of Jesus, did; she "kept in mind all these words, pondering them in her heart" (Lk. 2, 19). Father Laurentin has pointed out that St. Luke uses the Greek word *sumballo* for "ponder." This Greek word means literally "to throw together," and in our context "to match up" — "to ponder by comparing." No more appropriate word could have been employed, for it describes perfectly the Jewish and early Christian method of prayer. That prayer was a confrontation of one scriptural passage with another in order to understand more clearly a new event in Salvation History.

This method of confronting one text with another is as old as the Bible itself, and it continues to be the means the Church uses today in the Liturgy of the Word.

A. **From Adam to Christ: Messianic Hope**

1. **In the Beginning** . . . In the beginning of time God creates the world and all that is in it (1, 1a, 1b).* God climaxes His creative activity with the creation of Adam, and He rests on the seventh day (133). When the Lord God creates Adam (2), He perceives that "It is not good that man is alone . . . ," and so He creates a helper for Adam, called "woman." She shall be joined to man in marriage, and they become by this union "two in one flesh" (103). Man is perfectly happy in the garden, until a calamity occurs: led on by the tempter (139a, b), encouraged by Eve (108), Adam disobeys (50) and loses favor with God by sin (139). For his disobedience to God man must die (144) and must work by the sweat of his brow (124), but God makes a promise of victory and future redemption for the human race (3).

Sin grows worse in the world with the descendants of Adam: Cain

* Numbers in parentheses refer to the readings which follow in this book. The letters signify that the material spoken about is contained in the suggested supplementary readings in Appendix A.

murders his brother Abel (135). As time goes on man becomes so corrupt that God floods the earth, saving only Noe and his family (2a) in the Ark (86). Even after the Flood man continues to sin against his Creator, this time illustrated by the story of the Tower of Babel, where man is dispersed (94) for his pride (140).

The first eleven chapters of Genesis are a description of sin and its growth in the world. These stories of prehistory set the stage for the drama of salvation which now unfolds. We ask the question: How will the Lord God work out the salvation of a wicked race?

2. **The Call of the Chosen People.** To unite man once again with Himself God calls **Abraham** (5) around 1800 B.C., who becomes by this vocation the Father of the Chosen People (4). God orders him to leave his own country, leads him to the land of Chanaan, and enters into a covenant with him (38, 39a), promising him the land of Chanaan and descendants as numerous as the stars in the heavens and the sands on the sea. "In you shall all the nations of the earth be blessed" (Gn. 12, 3). God puts Abraham to a difficult test. He commands that he offer the human sacrifice of his only son and heir, **Isaac.** As Abraham is about to slay his beloved son, God intervenes, spares Isaac, and renews His promise to Abraham for his obedience (130a) and his faith (125).

The promise to Abraham is a high point in Salvation History. Only the covenant at Sinai and the covenant with David will compare with it. Only the Covenant through Jesus Christ will fulfill and surpass it. God assures Abraham and his numerous descendants of His constant protection and assistance in a land of promise, and above all through Abraham will come a blessing upon mankind — salvation for all believers (79a).

The promise to Abraham passes on to Isaac (5b), and to **Jacob** in his vision of the ladder (4, 5c). Jacob is named "Israel" by God and from his twelve sons (5d) will descend the Twelve Tribes of Israel. His beloved son, **Joseph** (4, 6), is sold into Egypt because of his brothers' jealousy (141) and God's providence. There he becomes, next to Pharaoh, the highest official in the land. When his brothers come to Egypt in search of food he eventually reveals his identity, receives them with joy and forgets past injury; he sends for his father Jacob (Israel) to come to the rich land of Egypt.

3. Redemption from Egypt and the Covenant at Mt. Sinai. For many generations the descendants of Israel live in Egypt, prospering in the rich land of Gesen, until the reign of the Pharaoh "who knew not Joseph." The Israelites have to endure cruel persecution at the hands of their overlords, which occasions their fervent prayer to the God of Abraham, Isaac, and Jacob for deliverance.

God hears the cry of His People and sends a liberator named **Moses** (7a). As a baby Moses is found by Pharaoh's daughter in a basket among the reeds on the river bank (86). Moses grows up in the royal court, but has to flee to the desert because of his sympathy for the Israelite cause. In the desert God appears to him in a burning bush, reveals His Name to Moses, and promises to renew His covenant with Israel (38). God commands Moses to return to Egypt and break the bonds of captive Israel. After casting nine plagues (7b) on the land, Moses tells the Israelites to prepare a lamb (53), eat it, and mark the doorposts of their homes with its blood, as a sign to the angel of the Lord that these homes belong to God's People. As a tenth plague God strikes down the first-born of all Egyptian families, but has the angel *pass over* the homes of the Israelites. This is the first Passover (7, 14, 96), and the king, defeated by the almighty power of the Lord, finally gives permission for the Israelites to leave Egypt.

Under the leadership of Moses the people march forth, guided by a fiery cloud (55, 55a). They pass dry-shod through the Red Sea (43, 91) as the Lord opens a way for them (48). They march into the desert (42b), are fed miraculously by God's provision of quail and manna (95), and overcome their desert enemies by God's power and Moses' intercession (120).

When Israel arrives at Mt. Sinai (Mt. Horeb), God comes down to the mountain in fire and thunder (15, 49). There He makes a new and wonderful covenant with them (8, 37): He forms them into His own Chosen People, a holy People (80), His beloved People (87). He is to be their God, they are to be His special People. Moses, lawgiver (8a, 51) and teacher, instructs the people in God's commandments (17, 131a) and tells them that God will always be loyal to His covenant-kindness if they keep His Law. When the ungrateful people fall into idolatry by worshiping the golden calf (8, 131), they repent of their sins, and God mercifully forgives them.

To ensure the holiness of Israel God promises His abiding presence in the Tabernacle (9, 54). He institutes laws of sacrifice, establishes the priesthood of Aaron (10, 101), and commands them to be holy, for He the Lord is holy (11). They must not hate one another, but love God (127) and their neighbor as themselves (128). Certain feasts are to be kept sacred forever to commemorate God's wonderful deliverance of His People: Tabernacles (13), Passover (14, 96), and Pentecost (15). Likewise they are to make a Day of Atonement every year for their sins against the Lord (12). The Sabbath is the great day set aside for worship and rest in imitation of God's rest after the work of creation (133).

4. **Journey Through the Desert and Conquest of the Promised Land.** After the events at Mt. Sinai, Israel sets out for the land promised to the patriarchs. In their journey through the desert (16), God tests His People to discipline them (44). They murmur against Moses and sin by revolt. God, who is slow to anger and rich in kindness, forgives them (98). He gives them water from the rock (57) and heals their wounds (74, 99). As a punishment for this stiff-necked people, however, He sentences them to wander forty years in the desert.

Josue (18a, 63) is appointed to succeed Moses and lead the people into the Promised Land (18). Moses promises that there will always by a prophet (60) in the land to guide them. He exhorts Israel on the Plains of Moab to keep the Lord's commandments; if they do, they will be the Lord's special People and will possess the land (17). God promises assistance to Josue in taking the land, and so Josue orders the people to break camp and cross the Jordan River. After crossing they storm and take Jericho by a miraculous intervention. At the end of his life of leading Israel against its enemies, Josue urges the people to keep the Law of Moses; if they obey, the Lord will continue to drive away their foes and give them rest.

The people continue to sin, however, and they are punished with defeat on all sides. At times God does raise up **Judges,** charismatic leaders like Gedeon, Samson, and Jephte (19), but disunity and sin triumph, and the land falls into the hands of the pagan Philistines.

5. **The Kingdom.** God raises up **Samuel** (21), prophet and last of the judges, but he is unable to unite Israel and defeat the Philistines. The people clamor for a king, and Samuel reluctantly grants their

wishes. God chooses **Saul** (22) from the tribe of Benjamin; Samuel anoints him and he becomes the first ruler over the newly-founded kingdom (88). At first the new king is successful in throwing back some of the enemy forces, but when popular favor passes to **David,** son of Jesse from the tribe of Juda, Saul grows envious (141).

When the proud King Saul disobeys God's commands, divine favor shifts to David (23). God commands the prophet Samuel to go to Bethlehem and secretly anoint David king (78). "The spirit of the Lord seized upon David from that day forward" (1 Sm. 16, 13). David slays the giant Philistine, Goliath (23a), and is now being acclaimed a greater warrior than the king himself. Saul cannot bear David's popularity and in a frenzy tries to kill the youth (141a), but David flees from his presence. Saul dies after a miserable life as king and a more miserable death in battle. David becomes king by God's choice and popular acclaim.

David conquers the Philistines at last, unites the land and the Twelve Tribes of Israel, captures Jerusalem and moves the capital there. He brings the Ark into the city in joyous procession (84, 107). David wants to build a temple to the Lord God and consults the prophet Nathan. In response Nathan tells David that David is not to build a house for God, but the Lord God will build an eternal home for David — an everlasting dynasty. With an oath God assures David that there will always be one of David's sons upon Israel's throne (65, 65a).

David is an ideal monarch until family troubles begin. He sins with Bathsheba and murders Urias (135), her husband. David is the first to admit his guilt, becoming a model for all future penitents. From this point on, however, everything seems to go wrong. Absalom, David's son, leads a revolt against his father, and even drives him from his capital. David is finally reinstated and on his death bed wills his kingdom to Solomon, his favorite son.

Under **Solomon** (24) the kingdom reaches its greatest glory. Solomon's greatest achievement is the building and solemn dedication of the Temple (54, 90). He extends the borders of the kingdom, carries on extensive commerce, is renown for his wisdom (24a) and administrative ability. The great king makes one mistake, however; he allows his many wives, permitted by the Law of Moses, to lead him into idolatry. His kingdom is grandiose but his religious convictions are weak. And so the Lord punishes His People devoted to idol-worship because of its king. At Solomon's death around 930 B.C., the kingdom is pitifully split into two independent parts, never to be reunited: into the kingdom of the north, called Israel, and the kingdom of the south, called Juda. The story of these two kingdoms is for centuries a continuous cycle of sin, punishment, repentance and forgiveness. God constantly warns — threatens — them through His spokesmen, the prophets, that He will punish them severely if they persist in their sins. He sends a long succession of prophets, promised by Moses (60), to His obstinate children. Each prophet receives a special preaching mission which can be generalized as: Repent of your sins, for the day of the Lord's punishment is near at hand! Sometimes the prophets are successful, but most of the time they go unheard.

Elias (25), prophet of God, preaches in the northern kingdom. He performs great wonders among the people, raising the son of the widow (48b, 56), challenging the 450 priests of the false god, Baal, and attacking evil in all forms. He opposes the idolatry, compromise, and avarice (141b) of the northern king, Ahab, and is forced by the murderous intentions of Queen Jezebel to flee south toward Mt. Sinai. There on the holy mountain the Lord God appears to him in a gentle breeze (49).

After Elias is taken by God to heaven in a fiery chariot, his mission is carried on by his follower and disciple, the prophet **Eliseus** (26), counselor and wonder-worker. He works great miracles in the land, such as the miraculous multiplication of the oil, the raising of the widow's son to life (56a) and the cure of the leper, Naaman (47).

Isaias (27) preaches in the southern kingdom during the eighth century. Called by God in a magnificent vision in the Temple, he pleads at the royal court at Jerusalem for conversion to the Lord from idolatry and sin. He threatens the House of Juda, the Vineyard of the Lord (89), with punishment if it will not repent. His message, however, is by no means all gloom. He foretells the day when all nations (81, 40a) will stream to Jerusalem, the mountain of the Lord. The Messias will come, born of a virgin (39, 106), a king like David (59), a prince of peace (66). This shoot from the root of Jesse shall be judge (147), and shall perform wonderful cures among the blind, the lame, and the deaf (46). Isaias' message is taken to heart by the good king Ezechias (27a), and the south is preserved from the collapse and final destruction which the Assyrian foe brings upon the northern kingdom in 721 B.C. Israel, the northern kingdom, is led into captivity, never to return. Now God's promises can be realized only in Juda.

Jeremias (28), a century later, preaches to Juda, which is totally corrupted by the scandalous (142a) King Manasses. Juda refuses to drink at the fountain of living water and turns to foreign streams. In God's name Jeremias pleads with his fellow Judaites to turn from their evil ways (118a), to repent especially of their idol-worship (131). If they do not repent, punishment is sure to follow. Josias (28a), a truly pious king, initiates a reform which is quite successful until his untimely death on the plains of battle. With this tragedy Juda slips into her old ways, Jeremias preaches in vain under persecution and oppression (73), and the darkest days in the story of salvation quickly approach.

The message of Jeremias does contain hope for the future. He foretells a messias, son of David (65a), a new covenant (38) in which perfect worship will be offered to God. God will make them once again His holy People, saving only a remnant (89a). Their sinful wounds can be cured, and God will heal them (48b, 100), so that once again they shall be His People, and He shall be their God. He foretells the destruction of Jerusalem (29) and predicts an exile. When the Exile comes about, he writes a letter to the captive Judaites that they should settle down in Babylon because it will be seventy years before they will return (31). According to the prophet's threat the Babylonians storm Jerusalem and a large number of the upper class is carried off to Babylon (598 B.C.).

Ezechiel (30) is God's prophet for those carried into exile. There he forecasts the destruction of Jerusalem and the punishment of those who remained in the sinful city. He consoles the exiles with the promise of restoration (30a) through a new covenant. God is punishing the wicked shepherd-kings of Juda and will raise up a good shepherd who will feed His flock with care and fidelity (58).

As prophesied the Babylonian armies come and sack the city, burn the Temple, carry off most of the population, and devastate the land. The destruction and **fall of Jerusalem** (587 B.C.) is a catastrophe unequaled in Old Testament times (29).

6. The Exile. As the prophets threatened, the Exile is God's way of chastising His People. Juda is carried off, the king is dethroned and taken into exile, the land is desolate and Jerusalem in ashes (29a). "How long, O Lord, how long?" In exile God's prophet Ezechiel makes every effort to console the Jews and to explain God's plan in scattering Juda, His beloved but sinful People.

Besides Ezechiel there is another prophet in the Exile, who preaches in the tradition of the great prophet Isaias; we shall call him **Second Isaias** because his prophecies begin with chapter 40 in the Book of Isaias. He proclaims wonderful things for the future (27b). There shall be a redemption (3) of God's People, accomplished by the Lord's Suffering Servant (27c, 72). The Good News (41) is near. The light is soon to dispel the darkness (55) when Israel shall have a new Exodus (31) to the Promised Land (148a). The Lord will come as a Judge (150a) and vindicate the rights of His Chosen People. "Come Lord! God of Israel, come! Deliver us from our oppressors!" At last the Lord God hears their prayer, for Cyrus the Persian decrees their return in 538 B.C.

7. The Jewish Community. Eighteen years after the Jews return from exile they begin the rebuilding of the Temple with the encouragement of the prophets Aggeus (90) and Zacharias. It is only five years after this (in 515 B.C.) that they dedicate the Temple (31).

In the following century Esdras the Scribe (32) and Nehemias (33), cup-bearer of the Persian king, come from Persia to help their brother-Jews. These pious men make heroic efforts to reform and rebuild the ruined city. Under Nehemias the walls are rebuilt, and under Esdras reforms are enacted and the covenant is renewed. But there is no longer a kingdom or a king. In time even prophecy ceases. The Jewish religion becomes centered around a strict observance of the Law, which is interpreted officially by the priests and scribes. In this period inspired wise men arise who develop previous revelation, enlighten the faithful, and purify their hopes.

The Jewish people never do regain their independence. They remain under the successive domination of the Persians, Greeks, Syrians, and finally the Romans. The only major uprising is that of the Machabean revolt against the Syrians in the second century B.C. In this revolt against the Syrian persecution of the Jews (35, 114, 123) a single family, the Machabees, manages to prevail over the enemy, chiefly because of a genuine religious fervor and fidelity to the Law of Moses (34). It is at this period that the Book of **Daniel** (36) consoles the persecuted and describes in figurative language the glorious reign of God at the end of time. The Son of Man (65b, 146, 149) will come from heaven upon the clouds to judge men and establish the kingdom of God.

At this stage in Salvation History the real heirs of the Old Testament faith are the **Poor of Israel** (83, 130), and not the Pharisees, scribes, and leaders of the land. These holy people — the oppressed, the meek, the humble — cry to God from their misery and beg God's deliverance by sending His Messias, promised by the prophets and awaited impatiently by the just.

B. **From the First Coming to the Second Coming of Jesus Christ**

1. **Jesus Christ, Saviour.** At last the Messias comes, fulfilling all of God's wonderful promises in the Old Testament. The Lord God is about to make a new and eternal covenant with His People (37). It happens in this way. God sends His angel Gabriel (36c) to Nazareth in Galilee, announcing to Mary, a virgin (39), that she is to become the Mother of the Messias (106) by the overshadowing of the Holy Spirit. Mary, the Mother of Jesus, becomes by this unparalleled event in Salvation History the Daughter of Sion (105), the Ark of the Covenant (167), for the Lord is with her. Her Son is to sit on the throne of David (65), ruling eternally over the kingdom of God (59), for He is the incarnate Word of God (62). The long-awaited Messias is about to come, realizing centuries of anxious hope ever since the days of Abraham, Moses, Jeremias (38), and the long line of Old Testament saints. Mary is the flowering of that hope, she is the perfection of the Old Testament preparation, the perfect "poor and humble one" (83).

Jesus is born in poverty (130) in Bethlehem and His first visitors are the "Poor of Israel," the shepherds (83a). With Him comes the only peace (66) that the world can ever realize. Magi (40) come from the east to visit Him; they come from among the Gentiles, foreshadowing the call of all men to the newly-sent salvation (81). "Born of a woman, born under the Law" (Gal. 4, 4), He obediently submits to the prescriptions of that Law (39a). Exiled to Egypt because of the jealousy of Herod, Jesus returns to Palestine, to the town of Nazareth, where under the care of Mary and Joseph (106a), His foster father, He grows in "wisdom and age and grace before God and men" (39b).

God prepares a great forerunner of the Messias in John the Baptist (38a, 42, 42a). He announces the coming of salvation, the coming of Jesus, the Lamb of God (53), who will baptize with water and the Holy Spirit (92). Jesus comes to John to be baptized (43), and from that moment the Baptist fades into obscurity, while Jesus begins God's great movement toward man to redeem him. Immediately after His baptism Jesus goes into the desert where He fasts for forty days and is tempted (44, 139b) by Satan (48a, 139a). Unlike the Israel of old (42b), He overcomes Satan and begins His preaching that the kingdom of God has arrived (41).

Like Moses (51) He gives a Law (131a, 131–138), a New Law which does not destroy the Old but fulfills it. This divine Teacher (51a) speaks with power and authority and not as the scribes and Pharisees. All admire His great wisdom (67), but the leaders of Israel are satisfied with the traditions of their forefathers, and have no need of the teaching of Christ. Jerusalem (84a) rejects the Anointed of God.

Unable to do anything with Israel as a whole, Jesus groups around Himself a few chosen men, who will become "fishers of men" (45c). After choosing these twelve apostles (45, 45a) He begins to teach them the mysteries of the kingdom of God. His Church is to be built on the firm foundation of these men (82). He chooses Simon, whom He names Peter (109), and announces that His Church will be built upon Peter, the Rock (110). He calls two other fishermen, John (113) and his brother James (113a). Nine others, too, He chooses, one of which is Judas, who will betray Him. He shows His three chosen ones, Peter, John, and James, His glory in the Transfiguration (9, 49), and they begin to wonder what sort of man this is.

"Who is this man?" He performs astonishing miracles over nature (48); He has power over the devils (48a); the power to cure sickness (48b, 99, 100), leprosy (47), blindness (48c); and even power over death itself (56, 56a, 48b, 145). This must be the Christ, this wonderful healer (46); but even more, He must be more than human, for He forgives sins and only God can forgive sins (97, 98).

Only gradually do the apostles come to know and understand Him and not completely so until the coming of the Holy Spirit, who teaches them all things. By stages do they come to know that this great Saviour sums up the whole Old-Testament preparation. He is the New Adam (50), who repairs the sins of mankind (2, 3). He fulfills the promises to Abraham and the patriarchs (4). This is the New Moses (51, 7a, 8a), the New Josue (63, 18a), who delivers His People, the New Israel, from captivity of sin and forms a New Covenant with them. This is the New Paschal Lamb (53), whose blood will redeem the People of God. He is the Rock (57) from which men will drink and receive everlasting life and refreshment. He even becomes the Bread of Life, the New Manna (95), which will feed His Church. As the Light of the World and the Pillar of Fire (55) He will allow none of His disciples to be overcome by darkness (55a). He also is the High Priest who atones (12) for the sins of the People. Greater than Solomon's Temple, He is the very Temple of God (54).

He is the epitome of perfection, possessing every perfection possible, human and divine. In Him is mercy (68) and love (69) for fallen man. His is a wisdom unequaled (67), a charity that knows no bounds (70), and a justice which will separate on the Last Day the good from the bad (71). In His patience He does not turn away from those who injure Him, but rather asks God's forgiveness for His persecutors (72).

So patient is this Servant of the Lord that He freely wills to lay down His life for fallen man : the Good Shepherd lays down His life for His sheep (58). He gathers together His beloved Twelve for the feast of the Passover and institutes the Passover of the new and eternal Covenant (38) at the Last Supper. He consoles them, as He announces His departure from this life, with the promise of the coming of the Holy Spirit (78a, 15, 93). He celebrates the Eucharist (95, 96), giving His own Body and Blood for the Sacrifice of the New Law (102). Having finished His work with the apostles, He now must suffer and die at the hands of sinners; and so with His apostles He goes to the Garden of Olives to pray and await the coming of His enemies.

His enemies come, led by Judas, who betrays Him with a kiss. They lead Him before the Jewish high priest, before the Roman procurator (59), before Herod of Galilee, and He is falsely accused (138) and sentenced to death (72a). He, the Eternal High Priest, now offers His sacrifice (101). Humiliated (129), He is lifted upon a cross (74) and there the Lamb of God (53, 14) suffers patiently (72) and dies (73) to atone (12) for the sins of the whole world. From His pierced side, from the side of the New Adam (50), springs forth, together with the blood (37) of the sacrifice, the water which foreshadows the gift of the Holy Spirit and the birth of the Church. Mary, the perfect member of the Church, joins in the sufferings of her Son and thereby fulfills her role as the New Eve (108), becoming at the same time the Mother of all believers (106). Jesus, the Son of God (62) lays down His life for the redemption of man, is taken down from the cross and placed in a tomb.

His body is not to know corruption, however, for according to His prophecy, He rises gloriously from the tomb on the third day (75, 75a). He appeared many times to His disciples (76, 61, 45b), gave them the power to forgive sins (97, 98) and the commission to teach all nations (81), and promising to send His Spirit He ascended into heaven forty days after the Resurrection (77, 77a).

2. **The Mystery of the Church.** Nine days after the Ascension, on the feast of Pentecost (15), Mary and the Eleven gather in the Upper Room. The Holy Spirit, promised by Jesus, comes upon the Church, anointing it (78), and witnessing to the truth of the preaching of the apostles. The disunity of the Tower of Babel is replaced by the unity of tongues (79, 94). It is the Apostle Peter (109) who is the head of the infant Church (110), and fearlessly he preaches the salvation of Israel in Jesus Christ (111). Many are gathered in Jerusalem for the great feast and it is to these that Peter proclaims that Jesus is the Lord, the Prophet (60), the Christ (64), who has suffered, died, and risen from the dead. "Repent and be baptized every one of you in the name of Jesus Christ for the forgiveness of your sins; and you will receive the gift of the Holy Spirit" (Acts 2, 38).

The Church, the Holy People of God (80), fulfills the aspirations of the old Israel. The Church brings salvation, for she is the Ark of salvation (86), purifying man by the waters of baptism (91). Her children are the spiritual sons of Abraham (79a). She is the New Kingdom (88), fulfilling the grandest expectations of the promises to David (23). She is the New Jerusalem (84), replacing the old (84a). The Church is the New Temple of God (54), greater than any temple in history (90). She is the Bride of Christ (87). Israel of old was

God's chosen vineyard, but failed and brought forth bad fruit; the New Israel is a vineyard, whose vinedresser is the Father; Christ is the Vine, and His followers are the branches (89). She is the Remnant (89a), composed of the meek and humble, the "Poor of Israel" (83, 83a, 130). Finally she is the extension of Christ in time, for the Church is His Mystical Body: Christ is the Head and His followers are the members of that body (85). Built on the firm foundation of the apostles (82), she brings salvation to all men (81, 40a, b), who will accept Christ. The office of deacon is established (101a) as the Church spreads rapidly. St. Paul preaches the Gospel to the Gentiles through the Mediterranean world and becomes the model of missionary work (112, 112a).

Jesus Christ does not leave His Church but continues His mission through the Spirit and the **Sacraments.** Those who do accept Christ must die to sin and rise with Christ (75a). They must be born again in the waters of baptism (91, 92, 91a, 57, 43), and be confirmed by the Spirit of God (93, 94). This new life is nourished by the Body and Blood of Christ in the Eucharist (95, 95a, 96); without the Bread of Life the Christian cannot have life in himself. If spiritually he becomes ill, he can receive Christ's forgiveness in the sacrament of penance (97, 98); and if physically he becomes ill, he can call in the elders of the Church and receive the sacrament of Holy Anointing (99, 100). Christ provides priests for His Church (101, 102) who share in His priesthood, acting as His instruments; and He raises matrimony (103) to the dignity of a sacrament, making it a type of His own love for His Spouse, the Church (104). This sevenfold sacramental gift that Christ confers on His Church is like a seven-branch stream coming from the side of Christ, for it is through His redemptive death and Resurrection that Christians have life.

3. **Christian Life.** Christian living means following Christ (118, 118a). For redeemed man, this is realized first in living with Christ in the Church, in receiving the sacraments and offering the sacrifice of the Church, the Mass. Life with Christ in the Church means hearing and acting on God's Word in the Scriptures (119). It means keeping the Commandments (131–8, 17) in a spirit of charity and sacrifice (131a). The Christian must practice the virtues, especially faith (125, 125a), hope (126), and charity (127, 128, 128a, b, c) and also humility (129), poverty (130), and obedience (130a). The

follower of Christ must be a man of prayer (120, 120a, 121). He must lead a life of mortification and fasting to obtain God's mercy and pardon for sin (122, 122a). The Christian has an obligation of setting a good example (123) both for his fellow Christians and for nonbelievers. He must lead a pure life, for he is a member of Christ's Body (136). He must work hard (124) for his own welfare and for the good of the community. He should see this life as a sojourn on his way to the promised land (13), confident that the Lord God will provide for him. In short, the Christian must be an imitator of Christ as were so many martyrs (114, 35), confessors (115), virgins (116), and holy women (117) in the history of God's People.

Living with Christ in the Church is man's best insurance against spiritual failure. Yet sin (139, 5a) always remains a threat in the spiritual life. The devil (139a) will never cease to tempt (139b) the members of the Church as he tempted Jesus Himself (44). Fallen man (2), redeemed by Christ (91, 3), is still prone to sin; he continues to be led to sin through the capital sins of pride (140), avarice (141b), lust (136), anger (141a), gluttony, envy (141) and sloth (142). God has created man in His own image and has more wonderfully re-created him by the redeeming work of His beloved Son. Thus the Christian, who shares in Christ's life in the sacraments, must ever be on his guard against every danger to Christian living: against scandal (142a), against an evil and lying tongue (143), against evil in every form, for sin has no place in Christ's kingdom and will not escape punishment.

4. The End of Time. Every man must die (144), and after death comes the judgment (146, 146a). Man will rise on the Last Day (145) and be judged by Jesus Christ (147, 40), the Just Judge (71), for either heaven (148, 148a), or for hell (149). All shall see Christ, the Son of Man (65b) on this Last Day as He comes once again in His glory (150, 150a, 77). Then shall His redemptive work be brought to completion; then shall the devil (139a) be cast down forever, and Satan's evil followers will be punished for their crimes against God (52). Then shall the elect of God be united in the Land of Promise (16), the New Jerusalem (84), a Kingdom of Light (55a). There the Bride of Christ (87), the Church, will be led to her spouse, Jesus Christ, to celebrate an eternal marriage feast (96) of the Lamb (53). This banquet of the just will be the glorious conclusion of God's loving plan to save man; it will conclude Salvation History with an everlasting union of happiness between God and His saints.

Come Lord Jesus! MaránaTha. Come!

PART TWO:
SCRIPTURE READINGS

1. CREATION IN GENESIS

Gn. 1, 1–13	Pss. 148, 1–14
Gn. 1, 14–23	103, 1–9
Gn. 1, 24–2, 3	18, 2–7
	8, 2–10

Introduction: God our Father speaks to us through His living Word. In this Scripture reading He communicates to us His teaching on creation. Let us be attentive as He tells us that in six days He created all things in the heavens and on the earth, that He specially created man, and that He rested on the seventh day. In preparation for our reading let us recite Psalm 148, verses 1–14.

First Reading: The Word of God as recorded in the Book of Genesis, chapter 1, verses 1–13. In this reading God is telling us that on the first three days He created the heavens and the earth, sea and land, and plants on the land.

⁋ In grateful response to the Word we have received, let us recite Psalm 103, verses 1–9.

Second Reading: The Word of God as recorded in the Book of Genesis, chapter 1, verses 14–23. In this reading God is telling us that on the fourth and fifth days He created the sun, moon, and stars; the fishes and the birds.

⁋ In grateful response to the Word we have received, let us recite Psalm 18, verses 2–7.

Third Reading: The Word of God as recorded in the Book of Genesis, chapter 1, verse 24 to chapter 2, verse 3. In this reading God is telling us that He created the animals and finally man; and that He rested on the seventh day.

⁋ In grateful response to the Word we have received, let us recite Psalm 8, verses 2–10.

Conclusion: Let us express our thanks to God for His creation of man and the universe by reciting the Our Father.

2. CREATION AND THE FALL OF MAN

Gn.	2,	4–9	Sir.	17,	1–8
	&	15–25	Sir.	17,	9–13
Gn.	3,	1–13	Pss.	50,	1–7
Gn.	6,	12–22		31,	1–7
Gn.	9,	8–17	Sir.	44,	17–18 (Douay 17–19)

Introduction: God, who rewards the just and punishes the evil, speaks to us through His living Word. In this Scripture reading He communicates to us His teaching on the creation and the fall of man. Let us be attentive as He tells us that He created our first parents and placed them in the Garden of Paradise, and that unfortunately they were tempted and fell into sin. As time passed the whole human race became sinful; so God destroyed the world with a flood, saving only Noe. In preparation for our reading let us recite Sirach 17, verses 1–8.

First Reading: The Word of God as recorded in the Book of Genesis, chapter 2, verses 4–9 and 15–25. In this reading God is telling us that He created our first parents and gave them the Garden of Paradise.

℄ In grateful response to the Word we have received, let us recite Sirach 17, verses 9–13.

Second Reading: The Word of God as recorded in the Book of Genesis, chapter 3, verses 1–13. In this reading God is telling us that the parents of the whole human race were tempted and fell into sin.

℄ In response to the Word we have received, let us recite Psalm 50, verses 1–7.

Third Reading: The Word of God as recorded in the Book of Genesis, chapter 6, verses 12–22. In this reading God is telling us that because of the great sins of mankind He had to destroy the world with a flood, saving only Noe and his family.

℄ In response to the Word we have received, let us recite Psalm 31, verses 1–7.

Fourth Reading: The Word of God as recorded in the Book of Genesis, chapter 9, verses 8–17. In this reading God is telling us that He promised Noe that He would never again destroy the world with a flood.

◖ In grateful response to the Word we have received, let us recite Sirach 44, verses 17–18.

Conclusion: Let us express our deep thanks to God for creating us and being merciful to us sinners by reciting this prayer:

O God, Creator of all things, despise not those who have sinned against You; rather, give us the grace of repentance that we may be sharers in the new Creation.

3. REDEMPTION

Gn.	3,	14–15	Pss.	129,	1–8
Is.	64,	1–12		85,	1–7
Eph.	1,	3–10	Is.	12,	1–6
			Ps.	30,	2–6

Introduction: In Sacred Scripture God is ever telling us of His Divine Word. In this Scripture reading He teaches us about the Redemption of mankind after Adam's sin. Let us be attentive as He tells us that the redemption, first announced in the Garden of Eden, was eagerly awaited by Israel and fulfilled in Jesus Christ. In preparation for our reading let us recite Psalm 129, verses 1–8.

First Reading: The Word of God as recorded in the Book of Genesis, chapter 3, verses 14–15. In this reading God is telling us that, when Adam sinned in the Garden, God cursed the serpent and gave mankind the first promise of victory over Satan.

◖ In grateful response to the Word we have received, let us recite Psalm 85, verses 1–7.

Second Reading: The Word of God as recorded in the Book of Isaias, chapter 64, verses 1–12. In this reading God is telling us that the prophet prayed fervently for the redemption of his people and the remission of their sins.

◖ In grateful response to the Word we have received let us recite the Canticle of Isaias from the Book of Isaias, chapter 12, verses 1–6.

Third Reading: The Word of God as recorded in the Epistle to the Ephesians, chapter 1, verses 3–10. In this reading God is telling us that St. Paul announced the Good News of salvation: "We have redemption in the blood of Christ, remission of sins, according to the riches of His grace."

℄ In grateful response to the Word we have received, let us recite Psalm 30, verses 2–6.

Conclusion: Let us thank God for His bountiful redemption in the blood of His Son by reciting this prayer:

O God, Saviour of mankind, You have restored a fallen people by redemption in the blood of Jesus Christ, Your Son; give us, we pray, an abundant share in the riches of His grace.

4. THE CALL OF THE CHOSEN PEOPLE

Gn. 12, 1–8	Pss. 94, 1–7
Gn. 28, 10–17	104, 1–11
Gn. 45, 1–20	134, 1–4
	104, 16–24

Introduction: God our Father instructs us through His living Word. In this Scripture reading He communicates to us His teaching on the call of the Chosen People. Let us be attentive as He tells us that He called Abraham to be the father of God's Chosen People, that the promise made to Abraham was handed down to Jacob and his descendants, and that Joseph won further security and safety for God's People in Egypt. In preparation for our reading let us recite Psalm 94, verses 1–7.

First Reading: The Word of God as recorded in the Book of Genesis, chapter 12, verses 1–8. In this reading God is telling us that He called Abraham who traveled to the land of Chanaan with his wife and relatives.

℄ In grateful response to the Word we have received, let us recite Psalm 104, verses 1–11.

Second Reading: The Word of God as recorded in the Book of Genesis, chapter 28, verses 10–17. In this reading God is telling us of Jacob's dream in which God promised to multiply Jacob's descendants.

℄ In grateful response to the Word we have received, let us recite Psalm 134, verses 1–4.

Third Reading: The Word of God as recorded in the Book of Genesis, chapter 45, verses 1–20. In this reading God is telling us how He sent Joseph into Egypt to preserve His Chosen People.

℄ In grateful response to the Word we have received, let us recite Psalm 104, verses 16–24.

Conclusion: Let us express our deep thanks to God for calling, preserving, and guiding His Chosen People by reciting this prayer:

May Your lasting mercy, O Lord, cleanse and defend Your Church; and since without You she cannot safely stand, may she be ever governed by Your grace.

5. ABRAHAM

Gn. 15, 1–15	Sir. 44, 19–23 (Douay, 20–27)
Gn. 18, 1–15	Ps. 127, 1–6
Gn. 22, 1–19	Lk. 1, 46–55
	Ps. 46, 2–10

Introduction: God our Father instructs us through His living Word. In this Scripture reading He teaches us about the Patriarch Abraham. Let us be attentive as He tells us that for his faith and obedience God rewarded Abraham with an eternal covenant by which he has become the father of all believers. In preparation for our reading let us recite Sirach 44, verses 19–23.

First Reading: The Word of God as recorded in the Book of Genesis, chapter 15, verses 1–15. In this reading God is telling us that His covenant with Abraham promised many blessings upon him and his numerous descendants.

℄ In grateful response to the Word we have received, let us recite Psalm 127, verses 1–6.

Second Reading: The Word of God as recorded in the Book of

Genesis, chapter 18, verses 1–15. In this reading God is telling us that He announced the birth of Isaac to Abraham and Sara.

¶ In grateful response to the Word we have received, let us recite the Canticle of Mary from the Gospel according to St. Luke, chapter 1, verses 46–55.

Third Reading: The Word of God as recorded in the Book of Genesis, chapter 22, verses 1–19. In this reading God is telling us that Abraham's greatest moment was his sublime act of obedience to God's command to sacrifice Isaac.

¶ In grateful response to the Word we have received, let us recite Psalm 46, verses 2–10.

Conclusion: Let us thank God for giving us our Father in the Faith, Abraham, and let us recite this prayer:

O God, You called Abraham out of a strange nation and made a perpetual promise with him; grant that we, his children in the faith, may be loyal to our call and faithful to Your commands.

6. JOSEPH

Gn.	39,	1–20	Sir.	44,	1–15
Gn.	41,	14–44	Pss.	118,	9–16
Gn.	50,	14–21		104,	16–22
				132,	1–3

Introduction: God our Father instructs us through His living Word. In this Scripture reading He teaches us about the Patriarch Joseph. Let us be attentive as He tells us how Joseph, sold into Egypt by his own brothers, became one of the most noble figures of the Bible. In preparation for our reading let us recite Sirach 44, verses 1–15.

First Reading: The Word of God as recorded in the Book of Genesis, chapter 39, verses 1–20. In this reading God is telling us how praiseworthy Joseph was in resisting the advances of the wife of his master.

¶ In grateful response to the Word we have received, let us recite Psalm 118, verses 9–16.

Second Reading: The Word of God as recorded in the Book of Genesis, chapter 41, verses 14–44. In this reading God is telling us how Joseph, by his God-given gift of interpreting dreams, became one of the highest officers in the land of Egypt.

¶ In grateful response to the Word we have received, let us recite Psalm 104, verses 16–22.

Third Reading: The Word of God as recorded in the Book of Genesis, chapter 50, verses 14–21. In this reading God is telling us how merciful Joseph was to his brothers, returning good for evil.

¶ In grateful response to the Word we have received, let us recite Psalm 132, verses 1–3.

Conclusion: Let us thank God for telling us about Joseph, patriarch and type of Christ, and let us recite this prayer:

O God, You chose Joseph the patriarch to be an Old-Testament model of virtue and piety; grant that we who admire his life may imitate his example.

7. ISRAEL'S DELIVERANCE FROM EGYPT

Ex. 3, 1–12	Pss. 135, 1–15
Ex. 12, 21–30	104, 23–27
Ex. 12, 31–42	104, 28–38
	113a, 1–8

Introduction: God our Father instructs us through His living Word. In this Scripture reading He communicates to us His teaching on Israel's deliverance from Egypt. Let us be attentive as He tells us that, under Moses' leadership, He terrified the Pharaoh by slaying the Egyptian first-born, and delivered the Israelites from the land of Egypt. In preparation for our reading let us recite Psalm 135, verses 1–15.

First Reading: The Word of God as recorded in the Book of Exodus, chapter 3, verses 1–12. In this reading God is telling us that He chose Moses to lead the children of Israel out of the land of Egypt.

¶ In grateful response to the Word we have received, let us recite Psalm 104, verses 23–27.

Second Reading: The Word of God as recorded in the Book of Exodus, chapter 12, verses 21–30. In this reading God is telling us that He destroyed the first-born of Egypt, but that He spared the Israelites.

¶ In grateful response to the Word we have received, let us recite Psalm 104, verses 28–38.

Third Reading: The Word of God as recorded in the Book of Exodus, chapter 12, verses 31–42. In this reading God is telling us that the Pharaoh, defeated by the Lord's power, sent the Israelites from Egypt.

¶ In grateful response to the Word we have received, let us recite Psalm 113a, verses 1–8.

Conclusion: Let us thank God for the deliverance of His Chosen People by reciting this prayer:

O God, who with a mighty hand and an outstretched arm delivered Israel from captivity, grant Your People, through Jesus Christ, redemption from sin and a place in Your heavenly kingdom.

8. THE ISRAELITES AT MOUNT SINAI

Ex. 19, 1–8	Pss.	17, 2–20
Ex. 24, 1–8		98, 1–9
Ex. 32, 1–14		116, 1–2
		105, 19–23

Introduction: God our Father instructs us through His living Word. In this Scripture reading He tells us about the Israelites at Mount Sinai. Let us be attentive as He describes some of the events which took place there when He made His covenant with Israel. In preparation for our reading let us recite Psalm 17, verses 2–20.

First Reading: The Word of God as recorded in the Book of Exodus, chapter 19, verses 1–8. In this reading God is telling us that the Israelites were His Chosen People, a Holy Nation.

¶ In grateful response to the Word we have received, let us recite Psalm 98, verses 1–9.

Second Reading: The Word of God as recorded in the Book of Exodus, chapter 24, verses 1–8. In this reading God is telling us that Moses read the Book of the Covenant, and that the people promised to be obedient. They affirmed this by offering a sacrifice.

¶ In grateful response to the Word we have received, let us recite Psalm 116, verses 1–2.

Third Reading: The Word of God as recorded in the Book of Exodus, chapter 32, verses 1–14. In this reading God is telling us that the Israelites broke the covenant by worshiping the golden calf.

¶ In response to the Word we have received, let us recite Psalm 105, verses 19–23.

Conclusion: Let us express our deep thanks to God for His instruction on the Israelites at Mount Sinai by reciting this prayer:

Be ever mindful of Your Covenant with Your People, O Lord God; and, though by our sins we are unfaithful servants, may we be always guided by Your abiding presence.

9. THE PRESENCE OF GOD IN THE CLOUD

Ex. 24, 12–18	Pss. 22, 1–6
Nm. 9, 15–23	26, 7–14
Mt. 17, 1–8	83, 2–8
	Lk. 2, 29–32

Introduction: God our Father instructs us through His living Word. In this Scripture reading He communicates to us His teaching on His presence among men. Let us be attentive as He tells us of His presence in the cloud which covered Mount Sinai, in the cloud over the Tabernacle in the desert, and in the cloud on the Mount of Transfiguration. In preparation for our reading let us recite Psalm 22, verses 1–6.

First Reading: The Word of God as recorded in the Book of Exodus, chapter 24, verses 12–18. In this reading God is telling us that He indicated His presence to Moses and the Israelites by a cloud which covered Mount Sinai.

¶ In grateful response to the Word we have received, let us recite Psalm 26, verses 7–14.

Second Reading: The Word of God as recorded in the Book of Numbers, chapter 9, verses 15–23. In this reading God is telling us that He showed to His Chosen People, by the cloud which covered the Tabernacle, that He was really present among them.

¶ In grateful response to the Word we have received, let us recite Psalm 83, verses 2–8.

Third Reading: The Word of God as recorded in the Gospel according to St. Matthew, chapter 17, verses 1–8. In this reading God is telling us that He again manifested His presence in a cloud at Jesus' Transfiguration.

¶ In grateful response to the Word we have received, let us recite the Canticle of Simeon from the Gospel according to St. Luke, chapter 2, verses 29–32.

Conclusion: Let us express our deep thanks to God for His abiding presence by this prayer:

Grant us, O Lord, a realization of Your constant presence within us, that, just as Israel knew You in the cloud, so we may be more aware that we are Your temples.

10. AARON

Ex. 29, 1–9
Nm. 17, 16–26 (Douay, 17, 1–13)
Nm. 20, 22–29

Sir. 45, 6–11 (Douay, 7–14)
Sir. 45, 12–15 (15–19)
Sir. 45, 16–19 (20–24)
Sir. 45, 20–22 (25–27)

Introduction: God our Father instructs us through His living Word. In this Scripture reading He teaches us about Aaron the priest. Let us be attentive as He tells us that Aaron and his sons alone were to be priests in Israel and that God confirmed Aaron's office with a miraculous sign. In preparation for our reading let us recite Sirach 45, verses 6–11.

First Reading: The Word of God as recorded in the Book of Exodus, chapter 29, verses 1–9. In this reading God is telling us that Aaron and his sons were to be consecrated priests by a special rite.

¶ In grateful response to the Word we have received, let us recite Sirach 45, verses 12–15.

Second Reading: The Word of God as recorded in the Book of Numbers, chapter 17, verses 16–26. In this reading God is telling us that Aaron's staff, a symbol of authority, sprouted as a sign to all Israel that the priesthood belonged to his family alone.

¶ In grateful response to the Word we have received, let us recite Sirach 45, verses 16–19.

Third Reading: The Word of God as recorded in the Book of Numbers, chapter 20, verses 22–29. In this reading God is telling us that Aaron died before entering the land of promise, and his priesthood was passed on to his son, Eleazar.

¶ In grateful response to the Word we have received, let us recite Sirach 45, verses 20–22.

Conclusion: Let us thank God for teaching us about Aaron the priest, and let us recite this prayer:

Almighty and eternal God, You established Aaron in the high priesthood to offer worship in the name of Your Holy People; grant that we who have an infinitely superior High Priest may join with Him in praise of You.

11. FROM THE BOOK OF LEVITICUS

Lv. 1, 1–9	Pss. 42, 1–5
Lv. 8, 1–13	133, 1–3
Lv. 19, 1–18	113b, 1–10
	111, 1–10

Introduction: God our Father instructs us through His living Word. In this Scripture reading He speaks to us through the Book of Leviticus. Let us be attentive as He tells us that Aaron and his sons, consecrated priests, must offer the sacrifices of the people, who are to be a holy people. In preparation for our reading let us recite Psalm 42, verses 1–5.

First Reading: The Word of God as recorded in the Book of Leviticus, chapter 1, verses 1–9. In this reading God is telling us that priests shall offer the sacrifices of the people.

℄ In grateful response to the Word we have received, let us recite Psalm 133, verses 1–3.

Second Reading: The Word of God as recorded in the Book of Leviticus, chapter 8, verses 1–13. In this reading God is telling us that Aaron and his sons were consecrated priests.

℄ In grateful response to the Word we have received, let us recite Psalm 113b, verses 1–10.

Third Reading: The Word of God as recorded in the Book of Leviticus, chapter 19, verses 1–18. In this reading God is telling us that His People must be holy.

℄ In grateful response to the Word we have received, let us recite Psalm 111, verses 1–10.

Conclusion: Let us express our deep thanks to God for His teaching in the Book of Leviticus with this prayer:

O Lord, You commanded the Israelite community: "Be holy, for I, the Lord your God, am holy"; give us, we pray, a share in the priesthood and sacrifice of the new Israel, that we may be sanctified in truth.

12. THE FEAST OF ATONEMENT

Lv.	16,	1–19	Pss.	65,	13–20
Mk.	15,	20–38		64,	2–6
Heb.	9,	1–14		21,	2–12
				46,	2–10

Introduction: God our Father instructs us through His living Word. In this Scripture reading He communicates to us His teaching on the Feast of Atonement. Let us be attentive as He tells us that in the Old Testament the blood of animals was offered every year to atone for the people's sins; and that in the New Testament Christ, the Eternal High Priest, shed His blood once and for all to atone for the sins of mankind. In preparation for our reading let us recite **Psalm** 65, verses 13–20.

First Reading: The Word of God as recorded in the Book of Leviticus, chapter 16, verses 1–19. In this reading God is telling us that once a year the high priest atoned for the sins of the people with the blood of animals.

℄ In grateful response to the Word we have received, let us recite Psalm 64, verses 2–6.

Second Reading: The Word of God as recorded in the Gospel according to St. Mark, chapter 15, verses 20–38. In this reading God is telling us that His only Son, Jesus, shed His blood on the cross for the sins of men.

℄ In grateful response to the Word we have received, let us recite Psalm 21, verses 2–12.

Third Reading: The Word of God as recorded in the Epistle to the Hebrews, chapter 9, verses 1–14. In this reading God is telling us that, because Jesus shed His blood once and for all on the cross, He is now Eternal High Priest in heaven.

℄ In grateful response to the Word we have received, let us recite Psalm 46, verses 2–10.

Conclusion: Let us thank God for the atonement which we have by the blood of Christ with this prayer:

Awake in us, O Lord, the spirit of repentance; and may we be cleansed of our sins by the bountiful atonement of Jesus Christ, High Priest.

13. THE FEAST OF TABERNACLES

Lv.	23, 33–43	Pss.	80,	2–6a
Neh.	8, 13–18		22,	1–6
Jn.	7, 37–39		121,	1–9
			106,	33–43

Introduction: God our Father speaks to us through His living

Word. In this Scripture reading He teaches us about the Feast of Tabernacles. Let us be attentive as He tells us that He commanded Israel to celebrate the feast of Tabernacles or Booths, that the feast was celebrated after the return from the Babylonian Exile, and that it was on the last day of this feast that Jesus proclaimed that He would refresh men with the gifts of the Holy Spirit. In preparation for our reading let us recite Psalm 80, verses 2–6a.

First Reading: The Word of God as recorded in the Book of Leviticus, chapter 23, verses 33–43. In this reading God is telling us that He commanded Israel to celebrate the Feast of Tabernacles to remind them how He cared for His People in the desert.

℄ In grateful response to the Word we have received, let us recite Psalm 22, verses 1–6.

Second Reading: The Word of God as recorded in the Book of Nehemias, chapter 8, verses 13–18. In this reading God is telling us that after the Babylonian Captivity He brought His people together in Jerusalem for the Feast of Tabernacles.

℄ In grateful response to the Word we have received, let us recite Psalm 121, verses 1–9.

Third Reading: The Word of God as recorded in the Gospel according to St. John, chapter 7, verses 37–39. In this reading God is telling us how, on the feast of Tabernacles, Christ announced that He would refresh men with the gift of the life of the Holy Spirit.

℄ In grateful response to the Word we have received, let us recite Psalm 106, verses 33–43.

Conclusion: Let us express our deep thanks to God for what He teaches us through the Feast of Tabernacles by reciting this prayer:

O God, our Father, who provided for Your chosen people in the desert, give us the rich gifts of the Spirit, that we may be assured of a place in the heavenly Jerusalem.

14. THE FEAST OF PASSOVER

Ex. 12, 21–28	Ps. 115,	1–10
Mt. 26, 17–30	Ex. 15,	1–10
Jn. 19, 28–36	Pss. 110,	1–10
	21,	12–19

Introduction: God our Father speaks to us through His living Word. In this Scripture reading He gives us His teachings on the Passover. Let us be attentive as He tells us that the angel spared — passed over — the Israelites whose doorposts were sprinkled with the blood of a lamb; and that this first Passover foreshadowed the Passover of the New Covenant, instituted at the Last Supper and fulfilled as the Lamb of God died upon the cross. In preparation for our reading let us recite Psalm 115, verses 1–10.

First Reading: The Word of God as recorded in the Book of Exodus, chapter 12, verses 21–28. In this reading God is telling us that the angel of death passed over the Israelites whose doorposts were sprinkled with the blood of a lamb.

¶ In grateful response to the Word we have received, let us recite the Canticle of Moses from the Book of Exodus, chapter 15, verses 1–10.

Second Reading: The Word of God as recorded in the Gospel according to St. Matthew, chapter 26, verses 17–30. In this reading God is telling us that, at the Last Supper, Christ celebrated the Passover of the New Testament.

¶ In grateful response to the Word we have received, let us recite Psalm 110, verses 1–10.

Third Reading: The Word of God as recorded in the Gospel according to St. John, chapter 19, verses 28–36. In this reading God is telling us that Christians are saved by the Lamb of God, whose bones, like those of the Passover lamb, were not broken.

¶ In grateful response to the Word we have received, let us recite Psalm 21, verses 12–19.

Conclusion: Let us express our deep thanks to God for Christ, our Passover, who had been offered for our salvation, by reciting this prayer:

O God, who redeemed mankind through the precious blood of Jesus Christ, Lamb of God, graciously grant that all who are bathed in the blood of the Lamb may be set free from the bonds of their sins.

15. THE FEAST OF PENTECOST

Ex.	19, 16–25	Pss.	28,	1–11	
Jn.	14, 23–29		103,	24–30	
Acts	2, 1–17	Jdt.	16,	13–17	(Douay, 15–21)
		Jl.	2,	28–32	

Introduction: God our Father instructs us through His living Word. In this Scripture reading He tells us about the Feast of Pentecost. Let us be attentive as He shows us that the coming of the Holy Spirit at Pentecost was foreshadowed by the Lord's coming in fire and thunder on Mount Sinai, was promised by Jesus at the Last Supper, and actually took place soon after the Lord's Ascension. In preparation for our reading let us recite Psalm 28, verses 1–11.

First Reading: The Word of God as recorded in the Book of Exodus, chapter 19, verses 16–25. In this reading God is telling us that He appeared to His Chosen People in fire and thunder on Mount Sinai.

℄ In grateful response to the Word we have received, let us recite Psalm 103, verses 24–30.

Second Reading: The Word of God as recorded in the Gospel according to St. John, chapter 14, verses 23–29. In this reading God is telling us that Jesus promised to send the Holy Spirit to His Chosen People of the New Law.

℄ In grateful response to the Word we have received, let us recite Judith 16, verses 13–17.

Third Reading: The Word of God as recorded in the Acts of the Apostles, chapter 2, verses 1–17. In this reading God is telling us that the Holy Spirit descended upon His Chosen People at Pentecost.

℄ In grateful response to the Word we have received, let us recite Joel 2, verses 28–32.

Conclusion: Let us express our deep thanks to God for Pentecost by reciting this prayer:

O God, You taught the faithful by sending the light of the Holy Spirit into their hearts; grant that, by the gift of the same Spirit, right judgment may be ours, and we may ever find joy in His comfort.

16. FROM THE BOOK OF NUMBERS

Nm. 10, 29–36	Pss. 113a, 1–8
Nm. 14, 1–24	67, 2–7
Nm. 27, 12–23	50, 3–14
	120, 1–8

Introduction: God our Father instructs us through His living Word. In this Scripture reading He teaches us through the Book of Numbers. Let us be attentive as He tells us that Moses led His Chosen People from Sinai toward the Promised Land, that He punished them severely for ingratitude and lack of faith, and that He appointed Josue to succeed Moses in leading the Israelites into the Promised Land. In preparation for our reading let us recite Psalm 113a, verses 1–8.

First Reading: The Word of God as recorded in the Book of Numbers, chapter 10, verses 29–36. In this reading God is telling us that Moses led His Chosen People from Sinai toward the Promised Land.

℄ In grateful response to the Word we have received, let us recite Psalm 67, verses 2–7.

Second Reading: The Word of God as recorded in the Book of Numbers, chapter 14, verses 1–24. In this reading God is telling us that He severely punished His people for ingratitude and lack of faith.

℄ In response to the Word we have received, let us recite Psalm 50, verses 3–14.

Third Reading: The Word of God as recorded in the Book of Numbers, chapter 27, verses 12–23. In this reading God is telling us that Moses was forbidden to enter the Promised Land and that Josue was appointed to succeed him.

⁋ In response to the Word we have received, let us recite Psalm 120, verses 1–8.

Conclusion: Let us express our deep thanks to God for instructing us through the Book of Numbers by reciting this prayer:

Arise, O God, and scatter our enemies; that, having overcome the temptations of this life, we may be brought, under the leadership of Your Son Jesus Christ, to the Promised Land of Your saints.

17. FROM THE BOOK OF DEUTERONOMY

Dt. 5, 1–21	Ps. 118, 1–8
Dt. 16, 1–17	118, 9–16
Dt. 28, 1–14	118, 57–64
	118, 129–136

Introduction: God our Father speaks to us through His living Word. In this Scripture reading He teaches us through the Book of Deuteronomy. Let us be attentive as He tells us that His People must always observe His Ten Commandments, that they must keep holy certain feasts throughout the year, and that great blessings will come upon them if they remain faithful to His teaching. In preparation for our reading let us recite Psalm 118, verses 1–8.

First Reading: The Word of God as recorded in the Book of Deuteronomy, chapter 5, verses 1–21. In this reading God is telling us that His People must learn and observe His Ten Commandments.

⁋ In grateful response to the Word we have received, let us recite Psalm 118, verses 9–16.

Second Reading: The Word of God as recorded in the Book of Deuteronomy, chapter 16, verses 1–17. In this reading God is telling us that His People must keep holy the great feasts of Passover, Pentecost, and Tabernacles.

⁋ In grateful response to the Word we have received, let us recite Psalm 118, verses 57–64.

Third Reading: The Word of God as recorded in the Book of Deuteronomy, chapter 28, verses 1–14. In this reading God is telling us that His Chosen People will receive great blessings if they are faithful to the Lord's teaching.

❡ In grateful response to the Word we have received, let us recite Psalm 118, verses 129–136.

Conclusion: Let us express our deep thanks to God for His teaching in the Book of Deuteronomy by reciting this prayer:

O God, You have ordered us to keep Your Commandments and walk in Your ways; give us a love for Your will and the grace to obey it.

18. FROM THE BOOK OF JOSUE

Jos. 1, 1–11	Pss. 43, 2–4
Jos. 6, 1–20	104, 7–11
Jos. 23, 1–11	43, 5–9
	77, 51–55

Introduction: God our Father instructs us through His living Word. In this Scripture reading He teaches us through the Book of Josue. Let us be attentive as He tells us that He fulfilled His promise to help Israel capture the Promised Land because they obeyed His laws. In preparation for our reading let us recite Psalm 43, verses 2–4.

First Reading: The Word of God as recorded in the Book of Josue, chapter 1, verses 1–11. In this reading God is telling us of His promise to aid the Israelites in crossing the Jordan.

❡ In grateful response to the Word we have received, let us recite Psalm 104, verses 7–11.

Second Reading: The Word of God as recorded in the Book of Josue, chapter 6, verses 1–20. In this reading God is telling us that He was faithful to His promise at the battle of Jerico.

❡ In grateful response to the Word we have received, let us recite Psalm 43, verses 5–9.

Third Reading: The Word of God as recorded in the Book of Josue, chapter 23, verses 1–11. In this reading God is telling us that He kept His promise to the Israelites because they obeyed His laws.

℄ In grateful response to the Word we have received, let us recite Psalm 77, verses 51–55.

Conclusion: Let us express our thanks to God for His faithfulness to His promises by offering this prayer:

Lord, God of Israel, under Josue You brought Your people through the River Jordan into the Land of Promise; may we, the New Israel, overcome our sins and enjoy the rich blessings of heaven.

19. FROM THE BOOK OF JUDGES

Jgs. 7, 9–22	Pss.	58, 2–6
Jgs. 12, 1–7		82, 14–19
Jgs. 16, 15–31		53, 3–9
		61, 2–9

Introduction: God our Father instructs us through His living Word. In this Scripture reading He tells us about three judges of the Old Testament. Let us be attentive as He shows us that He came to the aid of the judges of His people: Gedeon, Jephte, and Samson, to deliver His Chosen People from their enemies. In preparation for our reading let us recite Psalm 58, verses 2–6.

First Reading: The Word of God as recorded in the Book of Judges, chapter 7, verses 9–22. In this reading God is telling us that He gave His strength to Gedeon, who overcame His enemies.

℄ In grateful response to the Word we have received, let us recite Psalm 82, verses 14–19.

Second Reading: The Word of God as recorded in the Book of Judges, chapter 12, verses 1–7. In this reading God is telling us that He helped Jephte, the judge, when he called for God's help against the Ephraemites.

℄ In grateful response to the Word we have received, let us recite Psalm 53, verses 3–9.

Third Reading: The Word of God as recorded in the Book of Judges, chapter 16, verses 15–31. In this reading God is telling us that He restored Samson's strength in order to defeat His enemies, the Philistines.

¶ In grateful response to the Word we have received, let us recite Psalm 61, verses 2–9.

Conclusion: Let us sincerely thank God for teaching us through the Book of Judges to confide in His help by reciting this prayer:

Deliver the Church from its persecutors, O Lord our Judge, and grant us peace in our days, that we may enjoy the inheritance promised to Your saints.

20. RUTH

Ru. 1	Ps. 44, 11–18
Ru. 2	Prv. 31, 10–14
Ru. 3	Prv. 31, 15–23
Ru. 4	Prv. 31, 24–31
	Ps. 127, 1–6

Introduction: God our Father instructs us through His living Word. In this Scripture reading He tells us about the holy woman, Ruth. Let us be attentive as He shows us how good Ruth was to her mother-in-law, and how she became the wife of Boaz and an ancestor of David and Jesus Christ. In preparation for our reading let us recite Psalm 44, verses 11–18.

First Reading: The Word of God as recorded in the Book of Ruth, chapter 1. In this reading God is telling us how faithful Ruth was in returning to Bethlehem with her mother-in-law, Noemi.

¶ In grateful response to the Word we have received, let us recite the poem about the ideal wife from Proverbs 31, verses 10–14.

Second Reading: The Word of God as recorded in the Book of Ruth, chapter 2. In this reading God is telling us how Ruth met her future husband, Boaz.

¶ In grateful response to the Word we have received, let us recite Proverbs 31, verses 15–23.

Third Reading: The Word of God as recorded in the Book of Ruth, chapter 3. In this reading God is telling us that Ruth lay at Boaz's feet, claiming him for her husband by law.

¶ In grateful response to the Word we have received, let us recite Proverbs 31, verses 24–31.

Fourth Reading: The Word of God as recorded in the Book of Ruth, chapter 4. In this reading God is telling us that Boaz married Ruth who bore Obed, the grandfather of David and ancestor of Jesus Christ.

¶ In grateful response to the Word we have received, let us recite Psalm 127, verses 1–6.

Conclusion: Let us thank God for teaching us through the Book of Ruth by reciting this prayer:

O God, You have shown Your kindness in making Ruth the ancestor of Your Son, and Your greater kindness in making us His brothers; grant that we may live up to our noble state by a growing love for Your Gospel and a faithful observance of Your commands.

21. SAMUEL, PROPHET OF GOD

1 Sm. (1 Kgs.) 3, 1–19	Pss. 111, 1–10
1 Sm. (1 Kgs.) 9, 14–10, 1	98, 1–9
1 Sm. (1 Kgs.) 16, 1–13	19, 2–6
	88, 20–30

Introduction: God our Father speaks to us through His living Word. In this Scripture reading He tells us about the prophet Samuel. Let us be attentive as He shows us that He called Samuel to be a prophet; that Samuel anointed Saul the first king of Israel; and that, after Saul lost favor, Samuel anointed David the new king. In preparation for our reading let us recite Psalm 111, verses 1–10.

First Reading: The Word of God as recorded in the First Book of Samuel, chapter 3, verses 1–19. In this reading God is telling us that He called Samuel to be His prophet.

¶ In grateful response to the Word we have received, let us recite Psalm 98, verses 1–9.

Second Reading: The Word of God as recorded in the First Book of Samuel, chapter 9, verse 14 to chapter 10, verse 1. In this reading God is telling us that Samuel anointed Saul the first king of the Chosen People.

℄ In grateful response to the Word we have received, let us recite Psalm 19, verses 2–6.

Third Reading: The Word of God as recorded in the First Book of Samuel, chapter 16, verses 1–13. In this reading God is telling us that, because of Saul's disobedience, Samuel anointed David king.

℄ In grateful response to the Word we have received, let us recite Psalm 88, verses 20–30.

Conclusion: Let us thank God for the prophet and judge, Samuel, by reciting this prayer:

O God, You chose Samuel to be Your prophet in guiding the people of Israel; speak to us, we pray, through Your divine Word, for we Your servants are listening.

22. SAUL, FIRST KING OF ISRAEL

1 Sm. (1 Kgs.) 10, 17–25	Pss.	46, 2–10
1 Sm. (1 Kgs.) 18, 5–16		26, 1–3
1 Sm. (1 Kgs.) 31, 1–9		17, 21–31
		124, 1–5

Introduction: God our Father speaks to us through His living Word. In this Scripture reading He tells us about Saul, first king of Israel. Let us be attentive as He shows us that, in answer to Israel's plea for a king, He chose Saul to rule over Israel and protect them from their enemies. Yet, Saul's kingship and victories depended on obedience to God's commands; he failed and was punished with death. In preparation for our reading let us recite Psalm 46, verses 2–10.

First Reading: The Word of God as recorded in the First Book of Samuel, chapter 10, verses 17–25. In this reading God is telling us that Saul was proclaimed king — chosen from the tribe of Benjamin as the Lord's anointed.

¶ In grateful response to the Word we have received, let us recite Psalm 26, verses 1–3.

Second Reading: The Word of God as recorded in the First Book of Samuel, chapter 18, verses 5–16. In this reading God is telling us that David, because of his victory over the Philistines, became more popular in Israel than Saul.

¶ In grateful response to the Word we have received, let us recite Psalm 17, verses 21–31.

Third Reading: The Word of God as recorded in the First Book of Samuel, chapter 31, verses 1–9. In this reading God is telling us that, because of Saul's disobedience, his enemies overcame him.

¶ In response to the Word we have received, let us recite Psalm 124, verses 1–5.

Conclusion: Let us express our thanks to God for His providence over His People Israel by reciting the following prayer:

O God of justice and mercy, who rejected Saul and selected David king, by Your loving-kindness may we avoid a sentence of doom and enjoy the lot of Your elect.

23. DAVID

1 Sm. (1 Kgs.)	16,	1–13	Pss.	88, 20–30
1 Sm. (1 Kgs.)	17,	31–54		20, 2–8
2 Sm. (2 Kgs.)	7,	1–17		17, 32–39
3 Kgs.	2,	1–4		131, 11–13
				88, 35–38

Introduction: God our Father speaks to us through His living Word. In this Scripture reading He tells us about David. Let us be attentive as He shows us that He chose David and anointed him king, that He gave David power to kill Goliath, that David wanted to build a temple, and that he died leaving his kingdom to Solomon. In preparation for our reading let us recite Psalm 88, verses 20–30.

First Reading: The Word of God as recorded in the First Book of Samuel, chapter 16, verses 1–13. In this reading God is telling us that He chose and anointed king a young shepherd boy, David.

¶ In grateful response to the Word we have received, let us recite Psalm 20, verses 2–8.

Second Reading: The Word of God as recorded in the First Book of Samuel, chapter 17, verses 31–54. In this reading God is telling us that He gave David the power to kill Goliath.

¶ In grateful response to the Word we have received, let us recite Psalm 17, verses 32–39.

Third Reading: The Word of God as recorded in the Second Book of Samuel, chapter 7, verses 1–17. In this reading God is telling us that David wanted to build a temple; and that instead God would build an eternal house for David.

¶ In grateful response to the Word we have received, let us recite Psalm 131, verses 11–13.

Fourth Reading: The Word of God as recorded in the Third Book of Kings, chapter 2, verses 1–4. In this reading God is telling us that David, faithful to the Lord, died and left his throne to Solomon.

¶ In grateful response to the Word we have received, let us recite Psalm 88, verses 35–38.

Conclusion: Let us express our thanks to God for David, King of Israel and ancestor of Jesus Christ, by reciting this prayer:

O Lord God, You have fulfilled Your promises to David by sending an eternal King, Jesus Christ, Son of David; grant that we, His servants, may ever live in gratitude for Your loving-kindness and fidelity to David.

24. SOLOMON

3 Kgs.	1, 32–37	Ps.	71, 1–11
3 Kgs.	3, 5–15		71, 12–17
2 Chron. (2 Par.)	5, 1–10	Prv.	4, 1–13
		Ps.	47, 9–15

Introduction: God our Father speaks to us through His living Word. In this Scripture reading He tells us about Solomon, king of Israel. Let us be attentive as He shows us that Solomon succeeded

His father, David, as king of Israel; that he prayed for and received from God the gift of wisdom; and that he built and dedicated a great Temple, the dwelling place of God. In preparation for our reading let us recite Psalm 71, verses 1–11.

First Reading: The Word of God as recorded in the Third Book of Kings, chapter 1, verses 32–37. In this reading God is telling us that Solomon was appointed king of Israel to succeed his father, King David.

¶ In grateful response to the Word we have received, let us recite Psalm 71, verses 12–17.

Second Reading: The Word of God as recorded in the Third Book of Kings, chapter 3, verses 5–15. In this reading God is telling us that Solomon prayed for the gift of wisdom and received it from God.

¶ In grateful response to the Word we have received, let us recite Proverbs 4, verses 1–13.

Third Reading: The Word of God as recorded in the Second Book of Chronicles, chapter 5, verses 1–10. In this reading God is telling us that Solomon built and dedicated a great Temple, the dwelling place of God.

¶ In grateful response to the Word we have received, let us recite Psalm 47, verses 9–15.

Conclusion: Let us express our thanks to God for the wise King Solomon, builder of Israel's greatest Temple, by reciting this prayer:

Increase Your grace, O Lord, in the souls of Your humble servants; that while we now worship You in Your holy temple, we may one day, together with Your angels, rejoice in seeing You face to face.

25. ELIAS

3 Kgs. 17, 8–24	Pss. 1,	1–6
3 Kgs. 18, 21–39	6,	2–6
4 Kgs. 2, 1–11	Sir. 47,	24b–48, 5 (Douay, 48, 1–5)
	Sir. 48,	6–12a (48, 6–13a)

Introduction: God, who selects men to preach His Word, instructs us through that same Word. In this Scripture reading He tells us about the prophet Elias. Let us be attentive as He shows us some of the great events in the life of this holy man: how Elias raised the widow's son to life; how he discredited the false prophets of Israel; and how he was finally taken into heaven in a fiery chariot. In preparation for our reading let us recite Psalm 1, verses 1–6.

First Reading: The Word of God as recorded in the Third Book of Kings, chapter 17, verses 8–24. In this reading God is telling us that Elias, His prophet, was fed by the widow of Sidon and raised her son to life.

¶ In grateful response to the Word we have received, let us recite Psalm 6, verses 2–6.

Second Reading: The Word of God as recorded in the Third Book of Kings, chapter 18, verses 21–39. In this reading God is telling us that Elias challenged the false prophets to a contest and won.

¶ In grateful response to the Word we have received, let us recite Sirach 47, verse 24b to chapter 48, verse 5.

Third Reading: The Word of God as recorded in the Fourth Book of Kings, chapter 2, verses 1–11. In this reading God is telling us that Elias was taken to heaven at the end of his life in a fiery chariot.

¶ In grateful response to the Word we have received, let us recite Sirach 48, verses 6–12a.

Conclusion: Let us express our deep thanks to God for the great and holy prophet Elias by reciting this prayer:

We ask You, O Lord, that, as Elias was taken to heaven in a fiery chariot, so may we reach the land for which we long.

26. ELISEUS

3 Kgs. 19, 19–21	Pss. 99, 1–5
4 Kgs. 4, 1–7	15, 1–6
4 Kgs. 6, 8–23	Lk. 1, 46–53
	Sir. 48, 12b–14 (Douay, 13–15)

Introduction: God, who selects men to preach His Word, instructs us through that same Word. In this Scripture reading He tells us about Eliseus, the prophet. Let us be attentive as He describes for us the call of Eliseus and two miracles that the prophet performed. In preparation for our reading let us recite Psalm 99, verses 1–5.

First Reading: The Word of God as recorded in the Third Book of Kings, chapter 19, verses 19–21. In this reading God is telling us of the call of Eliseus by the prophet Elias.

℄ In grateful response to the Word we have received, let us recite Psalm 15, verses 1–6.

Second Reading: The Word of God as recorded in the Fourth Book of Kings, chapter 4, verses 1–7. In this reading God is telling us that Eliseus spared the widow and her son by the miraculous increase of oil.

℄ In grateful response to the Word we have received, let us recite the Canticle of Mary from the Gospel according to St. Luke, chapter 1, verses 46–53.

Third Reading: The Word of God as recorded in the Fourth Book of Kings, chapter 6, verses 8–23. In this reading God is telling us that Eliseus counseled the king of Israel against the enemy and performed a miracle to defeat them.

℄ In grateful response to the Word we have received, let us recite Sirach 48, verses 12b–14.

Conclusion: Let us express our deep thanks to God for Eliseus, the prophet, by reciting this prayer:

Create a new spirit in us, Lord God, by the wonderful workings of Your grace; and, as once Your prophet Eliseus worked wonders among Your People, so now may we confess our sins and serve You alone.

27. ISAIAS

Is. 6, 1–13	Is. 45, 15–25
Is. 1, 2–20	Is. 5, 18–24
Is. 11, 1–16	Is. 3, 1–8
	Is. 12, 1–6

Introduction: God, who selects men to preach His Word, instructs us through that same Word. In this Scripture reading He tells us about the Prophet Isaias. Let us be attentive as He tells us that Isaias, called to be a prophet in Israel, preached punishment and restoration for the People of God. In preparation for our reading let us recite the Canticle of Isaias from the Book of Isaias, chapter 45, verses 15–25.

First Reading: The Word of God as recorded in the Book of Isaias, chapter 6, verses 1–13. In this reading God is telling us that in a glorious Temple-vision Isaias saw the glory of God and received his call to preach to sinful Israel.

℄ In grateful response to the Word we have received, let us recite Isaias 5, verses 18–24.

Second Reading: The Word of God as recorded in the Book of Isaias, chapter 1, verses 2–20. In this reading God is telling us that Isaias charged Israel with sins as evil as those of Sodom and Gomorrha and pleaded with his people to repent.

℄ In response to the Word we have received, let us recite Isaias 3, verses 1–8.

Third Reading: The Word of God as recorded in the Book of Isaias, chapter 11, verses 1–16. In this reading God is telling us of Isaias' prophecy that after punishment there would come a new king, a new David, from the root of Jesse, who would rule over the remnant of Israel.

℄ In grateful response to the Word we have received, let us recite the Canticle of Isaias from the Book of Isaias, chapter 12, verses 1–6.

Conclusion: Let us express our deep thanks to God for teaching us through His prophet by reciting this prayer:

O God, through Isaias the prophet You promised redemption and fulfilled it in Your divine Son; grant that we, Your People, may receive deliverance from sin and the reward promised to those who follow that same Son, Jesus Christ, our Lord.

28. JEREMIAS

Jer. 1, 4–10	Pss. 21, 2–11
Jer. 37, 11–21	21, 12–19
Jer. 23, 1–8	21, 20–27
	21, 28–32

Introduction: God, who selects men to preach His Word, instructs us through that same Word. In this Scripture reading He teaches us about the prophet Jeremias, the man of sorrows. Let us be attentive as He tells us that He chose Jeremias to be His prophet from the beginning of his life; that Jeremias was persecuted bitterly for his prophecies of punishment; and that Jeremias preached a new king and a new redemption for Israel. In preparation for our reading let us recite Psalm 21, verses 2–11.

First Reading: The Word of God as recorded in the Book of Jeremias, chapter 1, verses 4–10. In this reading God is telling us that He chose Jeremias to be His prophet from the beginning of his life, "to wreck and to ruin, to build and to plant."

¶ In grateful response to the Word we have received, let us recite Psalm 21, verses 12–19.

Second Reading: The Word of God as recorded in the Book of Jeremias, chapter 37, verses 11–21. In this reading God is telling us that Jeremias was persecuted and cast into a pit because of his prophecies of punishment and destruction against wicked Jerusalem.

¶ In response to the Word we have received, let us recite Psalm 21, verses 20–27.

Third Reading: The Word of God as recorded in the Book of Jeremias, chapter 23, verses 1–8. In this reading God is telling us how Jeremias promised that after the punishment God would bless Israel with a new king and a new and more wonderful redemption.

¶ In grateful response to the Word we have received, let us recite Psalm 21, verses 28–32.

Conclusion: Let us thank God for teaching us about Jeremias the Prophet by reciting this prayer:

O God, whose will it was that Jeremias should prefigure in his sufferings the life of Your only-begotten Son, grant that we who have been redeemed by the Passion of Christ the King may be loyal to our calling.

29. THE FALL OF JERUSALEM (587 B.C.)

Jer.	6, 22–26	Lam.	1, 1–6
4 Kgs.	25, 8–12		1, 7–11
2 Chron. (2 Par.)	36, 18–21		1, 12–17
			1, 18–22

Introduction: God, who rewards the just and punishes the evil, speaks to us through His living Word. In this Scripture reading He teaches us about the fall of Jerusalem. Let us be attentive as He tells us how the prophet Jeremias had foretold this destruction by the king of Babylon, and how the beautiful Temple of Solomon was burned. In preparation for our reading let us recite Lamentation 1, verses 1–6.

First Reading: The Word of God as recorded in the Book of Jeremias, chapter 6, verses 22–26. In this reading God is telling us that the fall of Jerusalem was foretold by the prophet Jeremias.

¶ In response to the Word we have received, let us recite Lamentation 1, verses 7–11.

Second Reading: The Word of God as recorded in the Fourth Book of Kings, chapter 25, verses 8–12. In this reading God is telling us how the beautiful city of Jerusalem was captured and destroyed by the king of Babylon.

¶ In response to the Word we have received, let us recite Lamentation 1, verses 12–17.

Third Reading: The Word of God as recorded in the Second Book of Chronicles, chapter 36, verses 18–21. In this reading God is telling us of the destruction of the beautiful Temple that had been built by Solomon.

℄ In response to the Word we have received, let us recite Lamentation 1, verses 18–22.

Conclusion: Let us show our gratitude to God for His salutary teaching on the destruction of sinful Jerusalem by reciting this prayer:

Break for us, O Lord, we beg You, the bonds of sin, and mercifully turn away from us the punishment we have deserved.

30. EZECHIEL

Ez. 2, 1–3, 15	Pss. 87, 2–9
Ez. 7, 10–17	136, 1–6
Ez. 11, 13–21	88, 39–52
	Ez. 17, 22–24

Introduction: God, who selects men to preach His Word, instructs us through that same Word. In this Scripture reading He teaches us about Ezechiel, prophet of the Exile. Let us be attentive as He tells us that the mission of Ezechiel was to prophesy to the exiles in Babylon a day of doom and of ultimate restoration. In preparation for our reading let us recite Psalm 87, verses 2–9.

First Reading: The Word of God as recorded in the Book of Ezechiel, chapter 2, verse 1 to chapter 3, verse 15. In this reading God is telling us that He called Ezechiel to preach to the rebellious house of Israel in exile.

℄ In grateful response to the Word we have received, let us recite Psalm 136, verses 1–6.

Second Reading: The Word of God as recorded in the Book of Ezechiel, chapter 7, verses 10–17. In this reading God is telling us how Ezechiel preached a day of doom for Israel's sins.

℄ In response to the Word we have received, let us recite Psalm 88, verses 39–52.

Third Reading: The Word of God as recorded in the Book of Ezechiel, chapter 11, verses 13–21. In this reading God is telling us that Ezechiel also preached a day of restoration when the Lord would once again be their God and they His people.

℄ In grateful response to the Word we have received, let us recite Ezechiel 17, verses 22–24.

Conclusion: Let us recite this prayer in thanksgiving for God's teaching us about the prophet Ezechiel:

Through Your prophet, O Lord, You promised restoration, and through Your own Son You have accomplished it; grant that we Your exiles on earth may be gathered to Him our Shepherd in heaven.

31. THE RETURN FROM EXILE

Jer. 29, 4–14	Pss.	65, 1–12
Esd. 1, 1–11		12, 2–6
Is. 40, 1–11		129, 1–8
Esd. 6, 16–22		125, 1–6
		83, 2–8

Introduction: God, who rewards the just and punishes the evil, speaks to us through His living Word. In this Scripture reading He teaches us about the return from the Exile. Let us be attentive as He tells us of His promise to deliver the Israelites from captivity; of the fulfillment of His promise when, by the decree of Cyrus, He led His people through the desert to Jerusalem; and of the dedication of the new Temple for His worship. In preparation for our reading let us recite Psalm 65, verses 1–12.

First Reading: The Word of God as recorded in the Book of Jeremias, chapter 29, verses 4–14. In this reading God promises to free the Israelites from captivity.

℄ In grateful response to the Word we have received, let us recite Psalm 12, verses 2–6.

Second Reading: The Word of God as recorded in the Book of

Esdras, chapter 1, verses 1–11. In this reading God is telling us that by the decree of Cyrus, king of Persia, the Israelites were freed from captivity.

℄ In grateful response to the Word we have received, let us recite Psalm 129, verses 1–8.

Third Reading: The Word of God as recorded in the Book of Isaias, chapter 40, verses 1–11. In this reading God is telling us that He prepared the way for the return of the exiles through the desert.

℄ In grateful response to the Word we have received, let us recite Psalm 125, verses 1–6.

Fourth Reading: The Word of God as recorded in the Book of Esdras, chapter 6, verses 16–22. In this reading God is telling us that upon their return from exile the Israelites rebuilt and dedicated the Temple of God.

℄ In grateful response to the Word we have received, let us recite Psalm 83, verses 2–8.

Conclusion: Let us express our deep thanks to God for His deliverance of the Israelites from exile by reciting this prayer:

O Lord, guide and protector of those who hope in You, direct our every action and by Your providence bring us to the heavenly Jerusalem.

32. ESDRAS

Esd. 7, 1–28	Pss. 79, 2–8
Esd. 9, 1–15	79, 9–20
Neh. 8, 1–8	142, 1–6
	18, 8–15

Introduction: God our Father instructs us through His living Word. In this Scripture reading He teaches us about Esdras the Scribe. Let us be attentive as He tells us that Esdras, a pious Jew living in Persia, journeyed to Jerusalem about 100 years after the Babylonian Exile to effect religious reform among his people. In preparation for our reading let us recite Psalm 79, verses 2–8.

First Reading: The Word of God as recorded in the Book of Esdras, chapter 7, verses 1–28. In this reading God is telling us that Esdras received permission from the king of Persia to return to Jerusalem and restore religion and government which long after the Exile were still in a miserable state.

℄ In grateful response to the Word we have received, let us recite Psalm 79, verses 9–20.

Second Reading: The Word of God as recorded in the Book of Esdras, chapter 9, verses 1–15. In this reading God is telling us that Esdras prayed to God, after his return to Jerusalem, that the Lord might forgive the many sins of his people, especially marriages with idolatrous foreigners.

℄ In grateful response to the Word we have received, let us recite Psalm 142, verses 1–6.

Third Reading: The Word of God as recorded in the Book of Nehemias, chapter 8, verses 1–8. In this reading God is telling us that Esdras read and renewed the Law of Moses for all the people of Juda, who answered, "Amen, Amen."

℄ In grateful response to the Word we have received, let us recite Psalm 18, verses 8–15.

Conclusion: Let us thank God for teaching us about Esdras the Scribe, and let us recite this prayer:

O God, who raised up the holy Scribe, Esdras, to restore the spirit of religion to Your people, grant that we may continually enliven our faith by a fervent reading of Your holy Word.

33. NEHEMIAS

Neh. 1, 1–11		Lam.	2,	1–5
Neh. 2, 1–20		Lam.	2,	6–10
Neh. 6, 1–16		Pss.	50,	20–21
			147,	12–20

Introduction: God our Father instructs us through His living Word. In this Scripture reading He teaches us about Nehemias. Let us be attentive as He tells us that this cup-bearer for the king of Persia received a leave of absence about 100 years after the Babylonian Exile to return to Jerusalem and restore the ruined city. In preparation for our reading let us recite Lamentation 2, verses 1–5.

First Reading: The Word of God as recorded in the Book of Nehemias, chapter 1, verses 1–11. In this reading God is telling us that the broken-down state of Juda and Jerusalem was reported to Nehemias, who prayed to God for the restoration of his people.
¶ In response to the Word we have received, let us recite Lamentation 2, verses 6–10.

Second Reading: The Word of God as recorded in the Book of Nehemias, chapter 2, verses 1–20. In this reading God is telling us that, when Nehemias returned to Jerusalem and found the city in a state of desolation, he gathered the Jews together and began, with God's help, to rebuild the city.
¶ In grateful response to the Word we have received, let us recite Psalm 50, verses 20–21.

Third Reading: The Word of God as recorded in the Book of Nehemias, chapter 6, verses 1–16. In this reading God is telling us that Nehemias finished rebuilding the walls after bitter opposition from the surrounding peoples.
¶ In grateful response to the Word we have received, let us recite Psalm 147, verses 12–20.

Conclusion: Let us thank God for telling us about faithful Nehemias, and let us recite this prayer:

O God, You punished Your people when they sinned and blessed them when they obeyed; give us, we pray, a hatred for sin and a love for Your holy will.

34. FROM THE FIRST BOOK OF MACHABEES

1 Mc. 1, 21–29	Pss. 13, 1–7
1 Mc. 2, 15–28	59, 3–7
1 Mc. 3, 1–9	34, 1–9
	42, 1–5

Introduction: God, who rewards the just and punishes the evil, speaks to us through His living Word. In this Scripture reading He instructs us from the First Book of Machabees. Let us be attentive as He tells us how a single family, the Machabees, managed to prevail over the enemies of Israel, chiefly because of their genuine religious fervor and fidelity to the Law. In preparation for our reading let us recite Psalm 13, verses 1–7.

First Reading: The Word of God as recorded in the First Book of Machabees, chapter 1, verses 21–29. In this reading God is telling us how the pagan king profaned His holy Temple.

℄ In response to the Word we have received, let us recite Psalm 59, verses 3–7.

Second Reading: The Word of God as recorded in the First Book of Machabees, chapter 2, verses 15–28. In this reading God is telling us how Mathathias and his sons remained heroically faithful to His Law.

℄ In grateful response to the Word we have received, let us recite Psalm 34, verses 1–9.

Third Reading: The Word of God as recorded in the First Book of Machabees, chapter 3, verses 1–9. In this reading God is telling us how Judas, son of Mathathias, fought zealously to avenge the honor of God and His People.

℄ In grateful response to the Word we have received, let us recite Psalm 42, verses 1–5.

Conclusion: Let us thank God for His help to those who, like the Machabees, remain faithful to Him by reciting this prayer:

O God, our refuge and strength, fountain of all goodness, mercifully hear the fervent prayers of Your Church; and grant that what we ask with faith, we may surely obtain.

35. FROM THE SECOND BOOK OF MACHABEES

2 Mc. 7, 1–19	Pss. 118, 1–8
2 Mc. 7, 20–29	118, 153–160
2 Mc. 7, 30–42	93, 8–15
	118, 161–168

Introduction: God, who rewards the just and punishes the evil, speaks to us through His written Word. In this Scripture reading He shows us a beautiful example of fidelity to His Law in the Second Book of Machabees. Let us be attentive as He tells us how a mother and her seven sons suffered death rather than break His divine Law, so that they might be found worthy to rise to everlasting life on Judgment Day. In preparation for our reading let us recite Psalm 118, verses 1–8.

First Reading: The Word of God as recorded in the Second Book of Machabees, chapter 7, verses 1–19. In this reading God is telling us how six sons of a holy mother died, rather than break God's Law.
¶ In grateful response to the Word we have received, let us recite Psalm 118, verses 153–160.

Second Reading: The Word of God as recorded in the Second Book of Machabees, chapter 7, verses 20–29. In this reading God is telling us how this mother encouraged her seventh son to die for God's Law, that he might rise to everlasting life.
¶ In grateful response to the Word we have received, let us recite Psalm 93, verses 8–15.

Third Reading: The Word of God as recorded in the Second Book of Machabees, chapter 7, verses 30–42. In this reading God is telling us how this mother and her youngest son died, putting their hope in God's just judgment.
¶ In grateful response to the Word we have received, let us recite Psalm 118, verses 161–168.

Conclusion: Let us express our belief in God's teaching that, if we are faithful to His commands, we shall rise to everlasting life on the last day by reciting the Apostles' Creed.

36. FROM THE BOOK OF DANIEL

Dn. 1, 1–21	Dn. 3, 52–57
Dn. 6, 1–28	Dn. 3, 58–73
Dn. 14, 1–21	Dn. 3, 74–81
	Dn. 3, 82–90

Introduction: God our Father instructs us through His living Word. In this Scripture reading He teaches us from the Book of Daniel. Let us be attentive as He shows us how the example of Daniel was a constant source of encouragement to those who were so cruelly persecuted during the Machabean period of Jewish history. In preparation for our reading let us recite the Canticle of the Three Young Men from the Book of Daniel, chapter 3, verses 52–57.

First Reading: The Word of God as recorded in the Book of Daniel, chapter 1, verses 1–21. In this reading God is telling us that Daniel and his companions refused to break God's law by eating unclean food; for this God rewarded them with health and wisdom before the king.
℄ In grateful response to the Word we have received, let us recite Daniel 3, verses 58–73.

Second Reading: The Word of God as recorded in the Book of Daniel, chapter 6, verses 1–28. In this reading God is telling us that Daniel was cast into the lions' den for praying to the one, true God; God delivered Daniel from the lions and his enemies were punished.
℄ In grateful response to the Word we have received, let us recite Daniel 3, verses 74–81.

Third Reading: The Word of God as recorded in the Book of Daniel, chapter 14, verses 1–21. In this reading God is telling us that Daniel exposed the false worship of the idol Bel and had the priests of Bel put to death.
℄ In grateful response to the Word we have received, let us recite Daniel 3, verses 82–90.

Conclusion: Let us express our thanks to God for teaching us through the Book of Daniel by reciting this prayer:

O God, You delivered Daniel from his enemies because of his fidelity to Your law; grant that we, Your people, may suffer patiently with Christ, our Lord, and receive the rewards which You have promised.

37. THE NEW COVENANT

Ex.	24, 1–8		Pss.	24, 8–14
Lk.	22, 14–20			104, 1–11
Heb.	9, 11–22			137, 1–8
				102, 11–18

Introduction: God our Father instructs us through His living Word. In this Scripture reading He communicates to us His teaching on the New Covenant. Let us be attentive as He tells us that the Old Covenant, ratified by the shedding of the blood of animals, was fulfilled by Christ Himself, who sealed the New Covenant with His own blood. In preparation for our reading let us recite Psalm 24, verses 8–14.

First Reading: The Word of God as recorded in the Book of Exodus, chapter 24, verses 1–8. In this reading God is telling us of the Covenant of the Old Testament, sealed in the blood of animals.

℄ In grateful response to the Word we have received, let us recite Psalm 104, verses 1–11.

Second Reading: The Word of God as recorded in the Gospel according to St. Luke, chapter 22, verses 14–20. In this reading God is telling us of the New Covenant in the blood of Christ.

℄ In grateful response to the Word we have received, let us recite Psalm 137, verses 1–8.

Third Reading: The Word of God as recorded in the Epistle to the Hebrews, chapter 9, verses 11–22. In this reading God is telling us that the New Covenant fulfills the former Covenant because it has been sealed in the blood of Christ.

℄ In grateful response to the Word we have received, let us recite Psalm 102, verses 11–18.

Conclusion: Let us express our deep thanks to God for the New Covenant by this prayer:

O God, You made a covenant with Israel and fulfilled it with the saving blood of Jesus Christ; give us, we pray, a greater share in the New Covenant through the life-giving sacraments of Your Church.

38. THE NEW COVENANT

Gn.	17, 1–8		Ps.	49,	1–6
Ex.	5, 22–6, 8		Sir.	44,	19–21 (Douay, 20–23)
Jer.	31, 31–34		Pss.	104,	39–45
Mt.	26, 26–29			95,	1–13
				110,	1–10

Introduction: God our Father speaks to us through His living Word. In this Scripture reading He tells us about the New Covenant. Let us be attentive as He shows us that the Covenant which He established first through Abraham, then through Moses, was to be fulfilled and made perfect in the New Covenant by the blood of Christ. In preparation for our reading let us recite Psalm 49, verses 1–6.

First Reading: The Word of God as recorded in the Book of Genesis, chapter 17, verses 1–8. In this reading God is telling us of the Covenant He made with Abraham.

℄ In grateful response to the Word we have received, let us recite Sirach 44, verses 19–21.

Second Reading: The Word of God as recorded in the Book of Exodus, chapter 5, verse 22 to chapter 6, verse 8. In this reading God is telling us that He also made a Covenant with Israel through Moses.

℄ In grateful response to the Word we have received, let us recite Psalm 104, verses 39–45.

Third Reading: The Word of God as recorded in the Book of Jeremias, chapter 31, verses 31–34. In this reading God is telling us that He would give us a New Covenant.

¶ In grateful response to the Word we have received, let us recite Psalm 95, verses 1–13.

Fourth Reading: The Word of God as recorded in the Gospel according to St. Matthew, chapter 26, verses 26–29. In this reading God is telling us that at the Last Supper Christ established the New and eternal Covenant.

¶ In grateful response to the Word we have received, let us recite Psalm 110, verses 1–10.

Conclusion: Let us express our deep thanks to God for the New Covenant in Christ's blood by reciting the Our Father.

39. CHRIST, VIRGIN-BORN

Is.	7,	10–14	Pss.	97,	1–9
Mt.	1,	18–25		2,	1–7
Lk.	2,	1–7		88,	27–30
			Lk.	1,	46–55

Introduction: The Holy Spirit, who overshadowed the Virgin Mary, speaks to us through His written Word. In this Scripture reading He communicates to us His teaching on Christ, born of a virgin. Let us be attentive as He tells us that what the prophet Isaias foretold of a virgin bearing a child was announced to Joseph by the angel and fulfilled when the Virgin Mary brought forth Jesus, her first-born Son. In preparation for our reading let us recite Psalm 97, verses 1–9.

First Reading: The Word of God as recorded in the Book of Isaias, chapter 7, verses 10–14. In this reading God is telling us that a virgin would bring forth a son whose name would be called Emmanuel.

¶ In grateful response to the Word we have received, let us recite Psalm 2, verses 1–7.

Second Reading: The Word of God as recorded in the Gospel according to St. Matthew, chapter 1, verses 18–25. In this reading God is telling us that Mary is the virgin who would bear a son.

¶ In grateful response to the Word we have received, let us recite Psalm 88, verses 27–30.

Third Reading: The Word of God as recorded in the Gospel according to St. Luke, chapter 2, verses 1–7. In this reading God is telling us that the Virgin Mary gave birth to a son who is the Son of God.

¶ In grateful response to the Word we have received, let us recite the Canticle of Mary from the Gospel according to St. Luke, chapter 1, verses 46–55.

Conclusion: Let us thank God for giving us Jesus through the Virgin Mary by reciting this prayer:

O God, it was by Your will that the Word should become man, at the message of an angel, in the womb of the blessed Virgin Mary; grant to us, Your servants, that we who believe her to be truly the Mother of God may be helped by her intercession.

40. THE EPIPHANY OF JESUS

Mi. 5, 2–4	Pss. 98, 1–9
Mt. 2, 1–12	109, 1–7
Ap. 1, 4–8	71, 1–11
	46, 2–10

Introduction: God our Father speaks to us through His living Word. In this Scripture reading He gives us His teaching on the Epiphany or Manifestation of Jesus. Let us be attentive as He tells us that He appeared as Jesus Christ, born in Bethlehem, adored by Magi; and that He will appear again at the end of the world as our Judge. In preparation for our reading let us recite Psalm 98, verses 1–9.

First Reading: The Word of God as recorded in the Book of Micheas, chapter 5, verses 2–4. In this reading God is telling us of the coming Manifestation of a great and mighty King.

¶ In grateful response to the Word we have received, let us recite Psalm 109, verses 1–7.

Second Reading: The Word of God as recorded in the Gospel according to St. Matthew, chapter 2, verses 1–12. In this reading God is telling us of the Manifestation of Christ the King, adored by the Magi.

℄ In grateful response to the Word we have received, let us recite Psalm 71, verses 1–11.

Third Reading: The Word of God as recorded in the Apocalypse, chapter 1, verses 4–8. In this reading God is telling us that Christ, coming upon the clouds, will appear at the end of time.

℄ In grateful response to the Word we have received, let us recite Psalm 46, verses 2–10.

Conclusion: Let us express our thanks to God for the Epiphany of Jesus, His Son, by reciting this prayer:

O Lord, our God, You have revealed the birth of Your Son to the nations by a star; grant us this grace, that we who know You now by faith may after this life come to the vision of Your glory.

41. THE GOOD NEWS

Is.	52,	7–12	**Ps.**	147,	12–20
Mk.	1,	1–15	**Is.**	12,	1–6
1 Cor.	9,	16b–27	**Pss.**	114,	1–9
				8,	2–10

Introduction: God, who selects men to preach His Word, instructs us through that same Word. In this Scripture reading He communicates to us His teaching on the Good News of the Lord Jesus. Let us be attentive as He tells us that the Good News of salvation by Jesus Christ was awaited anxiously, demands our repentance and belief, and must be preached to others by word and example. In preparation for our reading let us recite Psalm 147, verses 12–20.

First Reading: The Word of God as recorded in the Book of Isaias, chapter 52, verses 7–12. In this reading God is telling us that Israel anxiously awaited the Good News that would bring salvation to all nations.

¶ In grateful response to the Word we have received, let us recite Isaias 12, verses 1–6.

Second Reading: The Word of God as recorded in the Gospel according to St. Mark, chapter 1, verses 1–15. In this reading God is telling us that Christ brought the Good News of salvation, telling us to repent and believe.

¶ In grateful response to the Word we have received, let us recite Psalm 114, verses 1–9.

Third Reading: The Word of God as recorded in the First Epistle to the Corinthians, chapter 9, verses 16b–27. In this reading God is telling us that St. Paul preached the Good News to others by word and example.

¶ In grateful response to the Word we have received, let us recite Psalm 8, verses 2–10.

Conclusion: Let us thank God for the Good News of the Lord Jesus by this prayer:

O Lord, our God, You have announced to fallen man the Good News of salvation and fulfilled it in Your Son; grant that by our faith and repentance we may be an example to others and receive the rewards promised by the Gospel.

42. ST. JOHN THE BAPTIST

Mal.	3,	1–5		Lk.	1,	76–79
Mt.	11,	2–15		Pss.	129,	5–8
Jn.	1,	19–34			1,	1–3
				Lk.	1,	68–75

Introduction: God, who selects men to preach His Word, instructs us through that same Word. In this Scripture reading He teaches us about St. John the Baptist. Let us be attentive as He tells us that St. John, whose coming was foretold in the Old Testament, announced to the Jews the coming of the Messias. In preparation for our reading let us recite the Canticle of Zachary from the Gospel according to St. Luke, chapter 1, verses 76–79.

First Reading: The Word of God as recorded in the Book of Malachias, chapter 3, verses 1–5. In this reading God is telling us that He will send a messenger who will prepare the way for His coming.

℄ In grateful response to the Word we have received, let us recite Psalm 129, verses 5–8.

Second Reading: The Word of God as recorded in the Gospel according to St. Matthew, chapter 11, verses 2–15. In this reading God is telling us that St. John the Baptist was the messenger who prepared the way for the coming of the Lord.

℄ In grateful response to the Word we have received, let us recite Psalm 1, verses 1–3.

Third Reading: The Word of God as recorded in the Gospel according to St. John, chapter 1, verses 19–34. In this reading God is telling us that St. John the Baptist fulfilled his role as God's messenger by pointing out that Jesus is the Son of God come into the world to save mankind.

℄ In grateful response to the Word we have received, let us recite the Canticle of Zachary from the Gospel according to St. Luke, chapter 1, verses 68–75.

Conclusion: In thanksgiving to God for sending St. John the Baptist, the forerunner of Christ, let us recite this prayer:

Almighty God, grant us, Your family, the grace to walk in the way of salvation; and by following the message of St. John may we be led safely to Him whose coming he foretold, Jesus Christ, Your Son, our Lord.

43. THE BAPTISM OF JESUS

Ex.	14, 21–31	Pss.	102, 1–10
Mt.	3, 1–17		105, 6–12
Acts	8, 35–39		65, 1–12
			31, 1–7

Introduction: God our Father speaks to us through His living Word. In this Scripture reading He instructs us on the baptism of

Jesus. Let us be attentive as He shows us that, just as Israel passed through the Red Sea, so Jesus was baptized in the Jordan. Christians share in this great act of redemption through the saving baptism of the Church. In preparation for our reading let us recite Psalm 102, verses 1–10.

First Reading: The Word of God as recorded in the Book of Exodus, chapter 14, verses 21–31. In this reading God is telling us that He miraculously saved the Israelites from the Egyptians by leading them through the Red Sea.

℄ In grateful response to the Word we have received, let us recite Psalm 105, verses 6–12.

Second Reading: The Word of God as recorded in the Gospel according to St. Matthew, chapter 3, verses 1–17. In this reading God is telling us of Jesus' baptism in the Jordan.

℄ In grateful response to the Word we have received, let us recite Psalm 65, verses 1–12.

Third Reading: The Word of God as recorded in the Acts of the Apostles, chapter 8, verses 35–39. In this reading God is telling us the story of the Ethiopian receiving the baptism of the Church, the same saving baptism that we receive.

℄ In grateful response to the Word we have received, let us recite Psalm 31, verses 1–7.

Conclusion: Let us express our deep thanks to God for baptism by reciting this prayer:

Almighty and merciful God, You have led Your people through the Red Sea, and Christ, Your Son, through the waters of baptism; may we, Your Church, be cleansed of our faults and by our baptism walk in newness of life.

44. THE TEMPTATIONS OF JESUS

Dt. 8, 1–10	Pss.	76, 2–13
Mt. 4, 1–11		77, 13–22
Jas. 1, 12–18		141, 2–8
	Sir.	2, 1–11 (Douay, 1–13)

Introduction: God our Father speaks to us through His living Word. In this Scripture reading He communicates to us His teaching on the temptations of Jesus. Let us be attentive as He tells us that the wandering of the Hebrew people for forty years in the desert, the trials of Jesus for forty days and nights in the wilderness, and the difficult journey of Christians in this world show us that through suffering and temptation we are made worthy of God's promises. In preparation for our reading let us recite Psalm 76, verses 2–13.

First Reading: The Word of God as recorded in the Book of Deuteronomy, chapter 8, verses 1–10. In this reading God is telling us that the Hebrew people were tested in the desert, but received blessings of bread and meat from heaven.

⁋ In grateful response to the Word we have received, let us recite Psalm 77, verses 13–22.

Second Reading: The Word of God as recorded in the Gospel according to St. Matthew, chapter 4, verses 1–11. In this reading God is telling us that the devil tempted Jesus three times in the wilderness, but Jesus did not give in.

⁋ In grateful response to the Word we have received, let us recite Psalm 141, verses 2–8.

Third Reading: The Word of God as recorded in the Epistle of St. James, chapter 1, verses 12–18. In this reading God is telling us that every Christian, like the Hebrews, and like Jesus, is tempted by the devil in his life.

⁋ In response to the Word we have received, let us recite Sirach 2, verses 1–11.

Conclusion: Let us ask God to help us in time of temptation by reciting the following prayer:

May the grace of Your Holy Spirit, we pray You, O Lord,

strengthen our wills, that by His help we may not be shaken by any temptation.

45. THE TWELVE APOSTLES

Jos. 4, 1–7	Pss.	112, 1–9
Mk. 3, 13–19		138, 1–13
Mt. 19, 27–29		132, 1–3
		88, 6–15

Introduction: God our Father speaks to us through His living Word. In this Scripture reading He communicates to us His teaching on the call of the twelve apostles. Let us be attentive as He tells us that just as the great liberator, Josue, in the Old Testament, chose twelve men, one from each tribe of Israel, to be his helpers in leading the people into the Promised Land; so Jesus, the Divine Liberator of the New Testament, chose twelve men to be His helpers in leading Christians to heaven. In preparation for our reading let us recite Psalm 112, verses 1–9.

First Reading: The Word of God as recorded in the Book of Josue, chapter 4, verses 1–7. In this reading God is telling us how Josue chose twelve men to build a monument out of twelve stones as a sign to all that God is with His People, protecting them from danger and leading them into the Promised Land.

℄ In grateful response to the Word we have received, let us recite Psalm 138, verses 1–13.

Second Reading: The Word of God as recorded in the Gospel according to St. Mark, chapter 3, verses 13–19. In this reading God is telling us that Jesus chose twelve men to be his helpers in building up His Church.

℄ In grateful response to the Word we have received, let us recite Psalm 132, verses 1–3.

Third Reading: The Word of God as recorded in the Gospel according to St. Matthew, chapter 19, verses 27–29. In this reading God is telling us about the great reward He has prepared for those twelve men who answered Jesus' call.

¶ In grateful response to the Word we have received, let us recite Psalm 88, verses 6–15.

Conclusion: Let us thank God for the call of the twelve apostles by reciting this prayer:

O God, Redeemer of fallen man, it was Your will to build Your Church upon the firm foundation of the twelve apostles; allow us, we pray, to imitate their example of leaving all and following Your Son, Jesus Christ, our Lord.

46. CHRIST THE DIVINE PHYSICIAN

Is.	35,	1–6	Pss.	146,	1–6
Mk.	1,	29–34		30,	20–25
Jn.	11,	14–44		144,	13b–21
				102,	1–5

Introduction: God our Father speaks to us through His living Word. In this Scripture reading He communicates to us His teaching on Christ the Divine Physician. Let us be attentive as He tells us that the work of the Divine Physician was foretold by the prophet Isaias and was fulfilled in the miracles of Christ, the greatest of which was the raising of Lazarus. In preparation for our reading let us recite Psalm 146, verses 1–6.

First Reading: The Word of God as recorded in the Book of Isaias, chapter 35, verses 1–6. In this reading God is telling us about Isaias' prophecy that the Divine Physician would work great cures.

¶ In grateful response to the Word we have received, let us recite Psalm 30, verses 20–25.

Second Reading: The Word of God as recorded in the Gospel according to St. Mark, chapter 1, verses 29–34. In this reading God is telling us that Christ, His Son, healed St. Peter's mother-in-law and many of the infirm that were brought to Him.

¶ In grateful response to the Word we have received, let us recite Psalm 144, verses 13b–21.

Third Reading: The Word of God as recorded in the Gospel according to St. John, chapter 11, verses 14–44. In this reading God is telling us of the most marvelous healing of the Divine Physician, the raising of Lazarus from the dead.

¶ In grateful response to the Word we have received, let us recite Psalm 102, verses 1–5.

Conclusion: Let us express our deep thanks to God for giving us Christ, our Divine Physician, by reciting this prayer:

O God and Father of us all, You have sent Your Son into the world to heal the sickness of a fallen race; may He cure us of our weakness and through the Divine Spirit give us lasting health of soul and body.

47. CHRIST'S POWER OVER LEPROSY

4 Kgs.	5,	1–14	Pss.	87,	2–10
Mt.	8,	1–4		116,	1–2
Lk.	17,	11–19		114,	1–9
				50,	1–14

Introduction: God our Father speaks to us through His living Word. In this Scripture reading God teaches us about His power to cure leprosy. Let us be attentive as He tells us about the cure of Naaman the leper by the prophet Eliseus, which foreshadowed the divine power of Jesus to cure lepers. In preparation for our reading let us recite Psalm 87, verses 2–10.

First Reading: The Word of God as recorded in the Fourth Book of Kings, chapter 5, verses 1–14. In this reading God is telling us that He miraculously cured Naaman the leper through His prophet Eliseus.

¶ In grateful response to the Word we have received, let us recite Psalm 116, verses 1–2.

Second Reading: The Word of God as recorded in the Gospel according to St. Matthew, chapter 8, verses 1–4. In this reading God is telling us that Jesus used His divine power to cure the leper who sought His aid.

℄ In grateful response to the Word we have received, let us recite Psalm 114, verses 1–9.

Third Reading: The Word of God as recorded in the Gospel according to St. Luke, chapter 17, verses 11–19. In this reading God is telling us that Jesus had mercy on the ten lepers and miraculously cured them.

℄ In grateful response to the Word we have received, let us recite Psalm 50, verses 1–14.

Conclusion: Let us ask God to cure us of our sickness and sin by reciting this prayer:

Watch over Your people, we pray You, O Lord, our God, and protect us from every infection of soul and body, that with clean minds and hearts we may praise You in the assembly of the saints.

48. THE POWER OF CHRIST OVER THE SEA

Ex. 14, 21–31	Ps. 106, 23–32
Mk. 4, 35–40	Ex. 15, 1–13
Mt. 14, 22–33	Pss. 45, 2–8
	88, 6–15

Introduction: God our Father speaks to us through His living Word. In this Scripture reading He communicates to us His teaching on the power of Christ over the sea. Let us be attentive as He tells us that the Lord God of the Old Testament showed His power over the sea when He delivered Israel through the Red Sea; that Christ, our Lord, has this same power as we see Him rebuke the wind and waves and even walk on the waters. In preparation for our reading let us recite Psalm 106, verses 23–32.

First Reading: The Word of God as recorded in the Book of Exodus, chapter 14, verses 21–31. In this reading God is telling us that He, the Lord God of Israel, had power to split the Red Sea open, so that His People might pass through to salvation.

℄ In grateful response to the Word we have received, let us recite the Canticle of Moses from the Book of Exodus, chapter 15, verses 1–13.

Second Reading: The Word of God as recorded in the Gospel according to St. Mark, chapter 4, verses 35–40. In this reading God is telling us that Christ, His Son, also has power over the sea as He calms the storm and saves His disciples.

℄ In grateful response to the Word we have received, let us recite Psalm 45, verses 2–8.

Third Reading: The Word of God as recorded in the Gospel according to St. Matthew, chapter 14, verses 22–33. In this reading God is telling us that Jesus, the Son of God, has complete control of the sea as He walks upon the waves.

℄ In grateful response to the Word we have received, let us recite Psalm 88, verses 6–15.

Conclusion: Let us ask God to save us by His almighty power:

Almighty God, whose right hand, so magnificent in power, split the waters of the Red Sea to save Israel from slavery, grant that Your all-powerful Son may calm the storms around us and give us lasting peace.

49. CHRIST TRANSFIGURED

Ex.	19, 16–25		Pss.	103, 1–4
3 Kgs.	19, 1–14			28, 1–11
Lk.	9, 28–36			10, 1–7
			Is.	42, 1–4

Introduction: God our Father speaks to us through His living Word. In this Scripture reading He communicates to us His teaching on Christ transfigured. Let us be attentive as He tells us that in His glory He appeared to Moses on Mount Sinai, and also to Elias on the same mountain. These manifestations of God's glory prepared for the Transfiguration of Jesus on the mountain. In preparation for our reading let us recite Psalm 103, verses 1–4.

First Reading: The Word of God as recorded in the Book of Exodus, chapter 19, verses 16–25. In this reading God is telling us that He appeared in His glory to Moses on Mount Sinai.

℄ In grateful response to the Word we have received, let us recite Psalm 28, verses 1–11.

Second Reading: The Word of God as recorded in the Third Book of Kings, chapter 19, verses 1–14. In this reading God is telling us that He appeared to Elias on Mount Horeb (Sinai).

℄ In grateful response to the Word we have received, let us recite Psalm 10, verses 1–7.

Third Reading: The Word of God as recorded in the Gospel according to St. Luke, chapter 9, verses 28–36. In this reading God is telling us that Christ, the Son of God, was transfigured on a high mountain before Peter, James, and John, and in the company of Moses and Elias.

℄ In grateful response to the Word we have received, let us recite Isaias 42, verses 1–4.

Conclusion: Let us express our deep thanks to God for the vision of Christ transfigured by reciting this prayer:

O God, in the glorious Transfiguration of Your only-begotten Son, the testimony of the prophets confirmed the mysteries of our faith; and Your voice, speaking out of a bright cloud, showed in a wonderful way that we are Your children; in Your mercy, we pray, make us co-heirs of Christ's kingdom and sharers in His glory.

50. CHRIST, THE NEW ADAM

Gn. 3, 1–24		Pss. 97, 1–9
Jn. 19, 25–30		129, 1–8
Rom. 5, 12–19		8, 2–10
		24, 8–15

Introduction: God our Father speaks to us through His living Word. In this Scripture reading He communicates to us His teaching on Jesus, the New Adam. Let us be attentive as He tells us that, as through Adam, the first man, sin entered the world, so through the death and Resurrection of Jesus, the New Adam, sin has been conquered and salvation brought to men. In preparation for our reading let us recite Psalm 97, verses 1–9.

First Reading: The Word of God as recorded in the Book of Genesis, chapter 3, verses 1–24. In this reading God is telling us that Adam, the father of the human race, brought death to mankind through his sin against God.

¶ In response to the Word we have received, let us recite Psalm 129, verses 1–8.

Second Reading: The Word of God as recorded in the Gospel according to St. John, chapter 19, verses 25–30. In this reading God is telling us that Jesus, the New Adam, died on the cross to bring salvation to man by conquering sin. Mary, the New Eve, stands at His side.

¶ In grateful response to the Word we have received, let us recite Psalm 8, verses 2–10.

Third Reading: The Word of God as recorded in the Epistle to the Romans, chapter 5, verses 12–19. In this reading God is telling us that, as through Adam sin entered the world, so through Jesus, the New Adam, sin has been conquered and grace restored to man.

¶ In grateful response to the Word we have received, let us recite Psalm 24, verses 8–15.

Conclusion: Let us express our deep thanks to God for giving us His Son as the New Adam by reciting this prayer:

O God, whose plan of salvation is to repair the damages of original sin by redemption in the blood of Your Son, we thank You for our baptism which blots out sin and makes us members of Christ, the New Adam.

51. CHRIST, THE NEW MOSES

Dt. 5, 1–21	Ps. 118, 33–40
Mt. 5, 1–17	118, 41–48
Heb. 3, 1–6	118, 49–56
	118, 57–64

Introduction: In Sacred Scripture God is ever telling us of His

Divine Word. In this Scripture reading He teaches us about Christ, the New Moses. Let us be attentive as He tells us that Moses on Mount Sinai received the Law from God; that Christ, the New Moses, in His Sermon on the Mount presented the charter for the New Law; and that Jesus Christ is superior to Moses. In preparation for our reading let us recite Psalm 118, verses 33–40.

First Reading: The Word of God as recorded in the Book of Deuteronomy, chapter 5, verses 1–21. In this reading God is telling us that on Mount Sinai Moses received the Law from God.

℃ In grateful response to the Word we have received, let us recite Psalm 118, verses 41–48.

Second Reading: The Word of God as recorded in the Gospel according to St. Matthew, chapter 5, verses 1–17. In this reading God is telling us that Christ, the New Moses, in His Sermon on the Mount presented the charter for the New Law.

℃ In grateful response to the Word we have received, let us recite Psalm 118, verses 49–56.

Third Reading: The Word of God as recorded in the Epistle to the Hebrews, chapter 3, verses 1–6. In this reading God is telling us that Jesus, the New Moses, is far superior to the Moses of old.

℃ In grateful response to the Word we have received, let us recite Psalm 118, verses 57–64.

Conclusion: Let us express our faith in Christ, our Teacher, the New Moses, by reciting the Apostles' Creed.

52. CHRIST, THE INCARNATE WORD OF GOD

Is. 55, 8–13
Jn. 1, 1–14
Ap. 19, 11–16

Ps. 32, 1–12
Sir. 24, 1–12 (Douay, 1–10)
Prv. 8, 22–36
Wis. 18, 14–16

Introduction: In Sacred Scripture God is ever telling us of His Divine Word. In this Scripture reading He communicates to us His teaching on Christ, the Incarnate Word of God. Let us be attentive as He tells us that He will send His Word down from heaven, that His Word has become flesh, or incarnate, and that all false teachers with their followers will be destroyed by the Word of God at the end of the world. In preparation for our reading let us recite Psalm 32, verses 1–12.

First Reading: The Word of God as recorded in the Book of Isaias, chapter 55, verses 8–13. In this reading God is telling us through His prophet, Isaias, that He will send His Word to us.

℄ In grateful response to the Word we have received, let us recite Sirach 24, verses 1–12.

Second Reading: The Word of God as recorded in the Gospel according to St. John, chapter 1, verses 1–14. In this reading God is telling us that He has sent His Word who has become flesh, or incarnate.

℄ In grateful response to the Word we have received, let us recite Proverbs 8, verses 22–36.

Third Reading: The Word of God as recorded in the Apocalypse, chapter 19, verses 11–16. In this reading God is telling us that at the end of the world all the false teachers and their followers will be destroyed by the Word of God.

℄ In grateful response to the Word we have received, let us recite Wisdom 18, verses 14–16.

Conclusion: Let us express our deep thanks to God for sending us His Incarnate Word, Jesus Christ, by reciting this prayer:

Grant, we pray You, almighty God, that we, who are bathed in the new light of Your Word-Made-Flesh, may show forth in our deeds the light that by faith shines in our hearts.

53. CHRIST, THE LAMB OF GOD

Ex.	12,	1–13	Is.	53,	1–7
Jn.	1,	29–37	Ps.	113a,	1–8
Ap.	7,	9–17	Is.	63,	1–4
			Ps.	95,	1–13

Introduction: In Sacred Scripture God is ever telling us of His Divine Word. In this Scripture reading He communicates to us His teaching on Christ, the Lamb of God. Let us be attentive as He tells us that, as the Passover lamb saved men from the slavery of Egypt, so Christ, the Lamb of God, saves men from the slavery of their sins that they may share in His heavenly glory. In preparation for our reading let us recite Isaias 53, verses 1–7.

First Reading: The Word of God as recorded in the Book of Exodus, chapter 12, verses 1–13. In this reading God is telling us that the Passover lamb saved men from the slavery of Egypt.

℄ In grateful response to the Word we have received, let us recite Psalm 113a, verses 1–8.

Second Reading: The Word of God as recorded in the Gospel according to St. John, chapter 1, verses 29–37. In this reading God is telling us that Christ, the Lamb of God, saves men from the slavery of their sins.

℄ In grateful response to the Word we have received, let us recite Isaias 63, verses 1–4.

Third Reading: The Word of God as recorded in the Apocalypse, chapter 7, verses 9–17. In this reading God is telling us of the glory which He has prepared for all whom Christ, the Lamb of God, has saved.

℄ In grateful response to the Word we have received, let us recite Psalm 95, verses 1–13.

Conclusion: Let us express our deep thanks to God for Christ, the Lamb of God, by reciting the Agnus Dei three times.

54. CHRIST, THE TEMPLE OF GOD

Ex.	33, 7–11	Pss. 83, 2–8
2 Chron. (2 Par.)	7, 1–3 & 12–16	14, 1–5
Jn.	2, 13–22	83, 9–13
		94, 1–7

Introduction: In Sacred Scripture God is ever telling us of His Divine Word. In this Scripture reading He communicates to us His teaching on Christ, the Temple of God. Let us be attentive as He tells us that, while He once dwelt in a tent in the wilderness, and later in the beautiful Temple at Jerusalem, now He dwells in Christ, His Son, the perfect Temple of God. In preparation for our reading let us recite Psalm 83, verses 2–8.

First Reading: The Word of God as recorded in the Book of Exodus, chapter 33, verses 7–11. In this reading God is telling us that at one time He dwelt among men in a tent in the desert.

¶ In grateful response to the Word we have received, let us recite Psalm 14, verses 1–5.

Second Reading: The Word of God as recorded in the Second Book of Chronicles, chapter 7, verses 1–3 and 12–16. In this reading God is telling us that He later dwelt in the Temple at Jerusalem.

¶ In grateful response to the Word we have received, let us recite Psalm 83, verses 9–13.

Third Reading: The Word of God as recorded in the Gospel according to St. John, chapter 2, verses 13–22. In this reading God is telling us that now He dwells in the perfect Temple, Christ our Lord.

¶ In grateful response to the Word we have received, let us recite Psalm 94, verses 1–7.

Conclusion: Let us express our deep thanks to God for Christ, the perfect Temple of God, by reciting this prayer:

O God, builder of spiritual houses, we beg You to unite us more closely to Your Son, Jesus Christ, by whose Resurrection we are built into the perfect Temple.

55. CHRIST, THE LIGHT OF THE WORLD

Ex. 13, 17–22	Pss. 26, 1–6
Is. 60, 1–5	42, 1–5
Jn. 9, 1–7	Is. 42, 5–9
	Ps. 35, 6–10

Introduction: In Sacred Scripture God is ever telling us of His Divine Word. In this Scripture reading He communicates to us His teaching on Christ, the Light of the World. Let us be attentive as He tells us that as Israel journeyed through the wilderness in the light of a pillar of fire, so too, Christ, fulfilling prophecy, is the Light of the World for the salvation of all men. In preparation for our reading let us recite Psalm 26, verses 1–6.

First Reading: The Word of God as recorded in the Book of Exodus, chapter 13, verses 17–22. In this reading God is telling us how the Israelites were led through the wilderness by means of a pillar of fire.

℄ In grateful response to the Word we have received, let us recite Psalm 42, verses 1–5.

Second Reading: The Word of God as recorded in the Book of Isaias, chapter 60, verses 1–5. In this reading God is telling us that He will come to enlighten the Gentiles.

℄ In grateful response to the Word we have received, let us recite Isaias 42, verses 5–9.

Third Reading: The Word of God as recorded in the Gospel according to St. John, chapter 9, verses 1–7. In this reading God is telling us that Christ proclaimed Himself the Light of the World.

℄ In grateful response to the Word we have received, let us recite Psalm 35, verses 6–10.

Conclusion: Let us express our deep thanks to God for giving us His Son, Jesus Christ, the Light of the World, by reciting this prayer:

O Lord, Saviour of fallen man, You led Israel to salvation by a pillar of fire; may Christ, Your Son, Light of the World, guide us from sin into the grace of Your presence.

56. JESUS CHRIST, LIFE-GIVER

3 Kgs.	17,	17–24	Wis.	3,	1–9
Lk.	7,	11–17	Pss.	114,	1–9
Jn.	11,	17–27		85,	1–13
			Is.	38,	15–20

Introduction: In Sacred Scripture God is ever telling us of His Divine Word. In this Scripture reading He communicates to us His teaching on Jesus Christ, the Life-Giver. Let us be attentive as He tells us that, as He gave life through the prophet Elias to the son of a widow, so also Jesus restored life to the son of the widow of Naim, and He further proclaimed before raising up Lazarus, "I am the resurrection and the life." In preparation for our reading let us recite Wisdom 3, verses 1–9.

First Reading: The Word of God as recorded in the Third Book of Kings, chapter 17, verses 17–24. In this reading God is telling us how He restored life to the son of a widow.

℄ In grateful response to the Word we have received, let us recite Psalm 114, verses 1–9.

Second Reading: The Word of God as recorded in the Gospel according to St. Luke, chapter 7, verses 11–17. In this reading God is telling us how Jesus gave life to the son of the widow of Naim.

℄ In grateful response to the Word we have received, let us recite Psalm 85, verses 1–13.

Third Reading: The Word of God as recorded in the Gospel according to St. John, chapter 11, verses 17–27. In this reading God is telling us that when Jesus raised Lazarus from the dead He proclaimed, "I am the resurrection and the life."

℄ In grateful response to the Word we have received, let us recite the Canticle of Ezechias from the Book of Isaias, chapter 38, verses 15–20.

Conclusion: Let us express our deep thanks to God for giving us life through Jesus Christ, our Life and Resurrection, by reciting this prayer:

Lord Jesus Christ, You raised the widow's son and gave him to his mother; we thank You for our life and membership in the Church through baptism, and we beg You to keep us always faithful to Your gifts.

57. CHRIST THE ROCK

Nm.	20,	2–11	Pss.	77,	1–8
Jn.	7,	37–39		77,	9–16
1 Cor.	10,	1–11	Is.	12,	1–6
			Ps.	41,	2–6

Introduction: In Sacred Scripture God is ever telling us of His Divine Word. In this Scripture reading He communicates to us His teaching on Christ the Rock. Let us be attentive as He tells us that the Israel of old drank from the rock in the desert; that Christ is the rock giving forth all-quenching water; and that, as the water from the rock saved the Israelites in the desert, so we are saved through Christ in the waters of baptism. In preparation for our reading let us recite Psalm 77, verses 1–8.

First Reading: The Word of God as recorded in the Book of Numbers, chapter 20, verses 2–11. In this reading God is telling us that the Israelites in the desert quenched their thirst by water from the rock.

℄ In grateful response to the Word we have received, let us recite Psalm 77, verses 9–16.

Second Reading: The Word of God as recorded in the Gospel according to St. John, chapter 7, verses 37–39. In this reading God is telling us that Christ is the rock giving forth all-quenching water.

℄ In grateful response to the Word we have received, let us recite the Canticle of Isaias from the Book of Isaias, chapter 12, verses 1–6.

Third Reading: The Word of God as recorded in the First Epistle to the Corinthians, chapter 10, verses 1–11. In this reading God is telling us that as the water from the rock saved and refreshed the Israelites in the desert, so we are saved and refreshed through Christ in the waters of baptism.

⸿ In grateful response to the Word we have received, let us recite Psalm 41, verses 2–6.

Conclusion: Let us express our deep thanks to God for Christ our Rock and our Saviour by reciting this prayer:

O Lord, our Rock, our Fortress, our Deliverer, graciously hear our prayer; and, as You quenched the thirst of Your People in the desert, so now refresh the souls of those who thirst for You.

58. THE GOOD SHEPHERD

Ez. 34, 11–31	Is. 40, 9–11
Lk. 15, 1–7	Ps. 79, 2–4
Jn. 10, 11–18	Jer. 31, 10–14
	Ps. 22, 1–6

Introduction: God our Father speaks to us through His living Word. In this Scripture reading He communicates to us His teaching on the Good Shepherd. Let us be attentive as He tells us that the coming of Christ, the Good Shepherd, was promised by the prophet Ezechiel, was pictured in the parable of the lost sheep, and was proclaimed to the world by Christ Himself. In preparation for our reading let us recite Isaias 40, verses 9–11.

First Reading: The Word of God as recorded in the Book of Ezechiel, chapter 34, verses 11–31. In this reading God is telling us that He will come to His People and care for them as a shepherd cares for his sheep.

⸿ In grateful response to the Word we have received, let us recite Psalm 79, verses 2–4.

Second Reading: The Word of God as recorded in the Gospel according to St. Luke, chapter 15, verses 1–7. In this reading God is telling us that His concern for us sinners is like that of a shepherd for lost sheep.

⸿ In grateful response to the Word we have received, let us recite the Canticle of Jeremias from the Book of Jeremias, chapter 31, verses 10–14.

Third Reading: The Word of God as recorded in the Gospel according to St. John, chapter 10, verses 11–18. In this reading God is telling us that Jesus Christ is the Divine Good Shepherd, who lays down His life for us, His sheep.

℄ In grateful response to the Word we have received, let us recite Psalm 22, verses 1–6.

Conclusion: Let us express our deep thanks to God for having sent His own Son to be our shepherd by reciting this prayer:

O Lord Jesus Christ, Good Shepherd, You laid down Your life for Your sheep; we, Your people and the sheep of Your pasture, humbly pray for guidance, that following You, our Shepherd on earth, we may be led to the pastures of eternal life.

59. CHRIST THE KING

Is. 9, 2–7		Pss. 60, 2–9
Lk. 1, 26–33		96, 1–12
Jn. 18, 33–40		71, 1–11
		97, 1–9

Introduction: In Sacred Scripture God is ever telling us of His Divine Word. In this Scripture reading He teaches us about Christ the King. Let us be attentive as He tells us that the kingship of Christ, foretold by the prophet Isaias, was announced by the angel to Mary, and was proclaimed by Jesus Himself in His trial before Pilate. In preparation for our reading let us recite Psalm 60, verses 2–9.

First Reading: The Word of God as recorded in the Book of Isaias, chapter 9, verses 2–7. In this reading God is telling us about a king who is to come in the future to rule an eternal kingdom.

℄ In grateful response to the Word we have received, let us recite Psalm 96, verses 1–12.

Second Reading: The Word of God as recorded in the Gospel according to St. Luke, chapter 1, verses 26–33. In this reading God is telling us that Mary will give birth to a King whose reign will have no end.

¶ In grateful response to the Word we have received, let us recite Psalm 71, verses 1–11.

Third Reading: The Word of God as recorded in the Gospel according to St. John, chapter 18, verses 33–40. In this reading God is telling us that Jesus Christ is a King whose kingdom is not of this world.

¶ In grateful response to the Word we have received, let us recite Psalm 97, verses 1–9.

Conclusion: Let us express our deep thanks to God for Christ our King by reciting this prayer:

Almighty, everlasting God, it is Your plan to make all things new in Your beloved Son, the universal king; grant in Your loving-kindness that all peoples of the earth, now torn apart by the wound of sin, may be subdued to the gentle rule of Him who is God.

60. CHRIST THE PROPHET

Dt.	18,	9–18	Ps.	117,	1–9
Jn.	6,	1–15		117,	10–18
Acts	3,	12–23		117,	19–25
				117,	26–29

Introduction: In Sacred Scripture God is ever telling us of His Divine Word. In this Scripture reading He communicates to us His teaching on Jesus Christ the Prophet. Let us be attentive as He tells us that Moses promised a prophet who would guide Israel, that Jesus Christ was recognized as the Prophet by the people, and that St. Peter preached that Christ the Prophet fulfilled the prophecy of Moses. In preparation for our reading let us recite Psalm 117, verses 1–9.

First Reading: The Word of God as recorded in the Book of Deuteronomy, chapter 18, verses 9–18. In this reading God is telling us that Moses promised a prophet like himself, whom the Lord would raise up to guide Israel.

¶ In grateful response to the Word we have received, let us recite Psalm 117, verses 10–18.

Second Reading: The Word of God as recorded in the Gospel according to St. John, chapter 6, verses 1–15. In this reading God is telling us that the people recognized Christ as the prophet promised by Moses.

℄ In grateful response to the Word we have received, let us recite Psalm 117, verses 19–25.

Third Reading: The Word of God as recorded in the Acts of the Apostles, chapter 3, verses 12–23. In this reading God is telling us that St. Peter preached that Christ is the prophet promised by Moses.

℄ In grateful response to the Word we have received, let us recite Psalm 117, verses 26–29.

Conclusion: Let us express our deep thanks to God for the gift of His Son, the greatest Prophet of all time, by reciting this prayer:

O God, who at sundry times and in divers manners spoke in times past to the fathers by the prophets, speak to us in our own day through Your Son, so that we, Your People, may know what is right and do it.

61. JESUS, AS THE LORD

Dt. 6, 4–19	Pss. 95, 1–13
Jn. 13, 1–15	18, 8–11
Jn. 20, 24–28	50, 9–14
	94, 1–7

Introduction: In Sacred Scripture God is ever telling us of His Divine Word. In this Scripture reading He communicates to us His teaching on Jesus as the Lord. Let us be attentive as He tells us that it was He, the Lord, who guided ancient Israel and gave her her laws; that He came to men as a humble servant in the person of the Lord Jesus; that after His Resurrection Jesus was worshiped as the Lord. In preparation for our reading let us recite Psalm 95, verses 1–13.

First Reading: The Word of God as recorded in the Book of

Deuteronomy, chapter 6, verses 4–19. In this reading God is telling us that He, the Lord, was the God of ancient Israel who directed His People and gave them laws to follow.

℄ In grateful response to the Word we have received, let us recite Psalm 18, verses 8–11.

Second Reading: The Word of God as recorded in the Gospel according to St. John, chapter 13, verses 1–15. In this reading God is telling us that, at the washing of the feet of His apostles, Jesus acknowledged the title "Lord."

℄ In grateful response to the Word we have received, let us recite Psalm 50, verses 9–14.

Third Reading: The Word of God as recorded in the Gospel according to St. John, chapter 20, verses 24–28. In this reading God is telling us that, after His Resurrection from the dead, Jesus was recognized as Lord and God by the doubting St. Thomas.

℄ In grateful response to the Word we have received, let us recite Psalm 94, verses 1–7.

Conclusion: Let us express our deep thanks to God for giving us Jesus, the Lord, by reciting three times:

Lord I am not worthy that You should enter under my roof; but say only the word, and my soul shall be healed.

62. JESUS, AS THE SON OF GOD

Mk.	1,	1–11	Prv.	8,	22–26
Mt.	17,	1–8	Pss.	109,	1–7
Mt.	27,	38–54		2,	1–9
				141,	2–8

Introduction: In Sacred Scripture God is ever telling us of His Divine Word. In this Scripture reading He communicates to us His teaching on Jesus, the Son of God. Let us be attentive as He tells us that at Jesus' baptism in the Jordan God called Him His Son; that when Jesus was transfigured on the mount, God again called Him His Son; and that when Jesus died on the cross He was proclaimed the Son of God. In preparation for our reading let us recite Proverbs 8, verses 22–26.

First Reading: The Word of God as recorded in the Gospel according to St. Mark, chapter 1, verses 1–11. In this reading God is telling us that when Jesus was baptized in the Jordan God Himself called Jesus His Son.

℄ In grateful response to the Word we have received, let us recite Psalm 109, verses 1–7.

Second Reading: The Word of God as recorded in the Gospel according to St. Matthew, chapter 17, verses 1–8. In this reading God is telling us that when Jesus was transfigured on the mount God again declared Jesus to be His Son.

℄ In grateful response to the Word we have received, let us recite Psalm 2, verses 1–9.

Third Reading: The Word of God as recorded in the Gospel according to St. Matthew, chapter 27, verses 38–54. In this reading God is telling us that even when Jesus was dying on the cross of Calvary He was proclaimed the Son of God.

℄ In grateful response to the Word we have received, let us recite Psalm 141, verses 2–8.

Conclusion: Let us express our faith in Jesus, the Son of God, by reciting the Apostles' Creed.

63. THE NAME "JESUS"

Nm.	27, 15–23		Pss.	112, 1–9
Mt.	1, 18–25			104, 1–11
Phil.	2, 5–11			102, 1–5
				137, 1–8

Introduction: In Sacred Scripture God is ever telling us of His Divine Word. In this Scripture reading He teaches us about the name "Jesus." Let us be attentive as He tells us that Josue, that is Jesus, was chosen to save God's People by leading them to the

Promised Land; that the name "Jesus" was given to our Lord to describe His mission of saving His People from their sins; and that this name has been given the highest honor of any name in heaven or on earth. In preparation for our reading let us recite Psalm 112, verses 1–9.

First Reading: The Word of God as recorded in the Book of Numbers, chapter 27, verses 15–23. In this reading God is telling us that Josue, also called Jesus, was chosen to save God's People by leading them into the Promised Land.

℄ In grateful response to the Word we have received, let us recite Psalm 104, verses 1–11.

Second Reading: The Word of God as recorded in the Gospel according to St. Matthew, chapter 1, verses 18–25. In this reading God is telling us the name "Jesus" was given to our Lord to describe His mission on earth of saving His People from their sins.

℄ In grateful response to the Word we have received, let us recite Psalm 102, verses 1–5.

Third Reading: The Word of God as recorded in the Epistle to the Philippians, chapter 2, verses 5–11. In this reading God is telling us that, because of our Lord's redeeming work, the name of Jesus is given the highest honor of any name on earth or in heaven.

℄ In grateful response to the Word we have received, let us recite Psalm 137, verses 1–8.

Conclusion: Let us express our deep thanks to God for teaching us about the holy name of Jesus by reciting this prayer:

O God, You appointed Your only-begotten Son to be the Saviour of mankind and commanded that His name should be Jesus; grant us this grace, that we may enjoy the vision of Him in heaven whose holy name we honor on earth.

64. JESUS' NAME "CHRIST"

Lk.	9, 18–22		Is.	61,	1–3
Mk.	14, 53–65		Pss.	44,	2–10
Acts	2, 22–41			88,	47–52
				15,	1–11

Introduction: In Sacred Scripture God is ever telling us of His Divine Word. In this Scripture reading He teaches us about Jesus' name "Christ," which means "Messias." Let us be attentive as He tells us through St. Peter's confession that Jesus is the Christ, the Son of the living God; that before the Jewish rulers Jesus admitted He was the Christ; and that St. Peter bears witness that Jesus is the Christ by reason of His Passion, death, and Resurrection. In preparation for our reading let us recite Isaias 61, verses 1–3.

First Reading: The Word of God as recorded in the Gospel according to St. Luke, chapter 9, verses 18–22. In this reading God is telling us that Peter, having seen all the wonderful things Jesus did, confessed that Jesus is the Christ.

¶ In grateful response to the Word we have received, let us recite Psalm 44, verses 2–10.

Second Reading: The Word of God as recorded in the Gospel according to St. Mark, chapter 14, verses 53–65. In this reading God is telling us that Jesus, in the trial before His death, told the rulers of the Jewish people that He was their Christ or Messias.

¶ In grateful response to the Word we have received, let us recite Psalm 88, verses 47–52.

Third Reading: The Word of God as recorded in the Acts of the Apostles, chapter 2, verses 22–41. In this reading God is telling us that Jesus, by His Passion, death, and Resurrection, is truly the Christ.

¶ In grateful response to the Word we have received, let us recite Psalm 15, verses 1–11.

Conclusion: Let us express our deep thanks to God for telling us about Jesus' name "Christ" by reciting the Kyrie and Christe as we do at Mass.

65. JESUS CHRIST, SON OF DAVID

2 Sm. (2 Kgs.)	7, 4–17		Pss.	71, 1–11
Lk.	1, 26–33			88, 20–30
Mt.	21, 1–11		Za.	9, 9–10
			Ps.	117, 19–29

Introduction: In Sacred Scripture God is ever telling us of His Divine Word. In this Scripture reading He communicates to us His teaching on Jesus Christ, Son of David. Let us be attentive as He tells us that He promised King David a descendant to rule his kingdom forever; that Jesus was born of the line of David; and that Jesus accepted the title when the people hailed Him as Son of David. In preparation for our reading let us recite Psalm 71, verses 1–11.

First Reading: The Word of God as recorded in the Second Book of Samuel, chapter 7, verses 4–17. In this reading God is telling us that He promised King David a descendant to rule his kingdom forever.

¶ In grateful response to the Word we have received, let us recite Psalm 88, verses 20–30.

Second Reading: The Word of God as recorded in the Gospel according to St. Luke, chapter 1, verses 26–33. In this reading God is telling us that Jesus was born of the line of David.

¶ In grateful response to the Word we have received, let us recite Zacharias 9, verses 9–10.

Third Reading: The Word of God as recorded in the Gospel according to St. Matthew, chapter 21, verses 1–11. In this reading God is telling us that Jesus accepted the title "Son of David" when the people hailed Him as such.

¶ In grateful response to the Word we have received, let us recite Psalm 117, verses 19–29.

Conclusion: Let us express our deep thanks to God for Jesus Christ, Son of David, by reciting this prayer:

O God, You told David that he should not build a house for You, but rather You would build one for him; grant that Your Son, Jesus Christ, Son of David, the fulfillment of prophecy, may bless us, the members of His household, and give us a large share in the graces of His redemption.

66. CHRIST, THE PRINCE OF PEACE

Is.	9,	2–7	Ps.	121,	1–9
Lk.	2,	8–14	Is.	52,	7–9
Jn.	20,	19–29	Pss.	8,	2–10
				84,	9–14

Introduction: In Sacred Scripture God is ever telling us of His Divine Word. In this Scripture reading He communicates to us His teaching on Christ, the Prince of Peace. Let us be attentive as He tells us that the Messias who was to come would be the Prince of Peace; that the angels announced on the night of Christ's birth that He brought peace to all men; and that peace comes to us principally in the Resurrection of our Lord. In preparation for our reading let us recite Psalm 121, verses 1–9.

First Reading: The Word of God as recorded in the Book of Isaias, chapter 9, verses 2–7. In this reading God is telling us through His prophet that the Christ-to-come would be the Prince of Peace.

¶ In grateful response to the Word we have received, let us recite Isaias 52, verses 7–9.

Second Reading: The Word of God as recorded in the Gospel according to St. Luke, chapter 2, verses 8–14. In this reading God is telling us that with the birth of Christ peace came to men, and the angels announced it to the shepherds.

¶ In grateful response to the Word we have received, let us recite Psalm 8, verses 2–10.

Third Reading: The Word of God as recorded in the Gospel according to St. John, chapter 20, verses 19–29. In this reading God is telling us that with the Resurrection of Christ peace comes to us in the fullest measure possible.

¶ In grateful response to the Word we have received, let us recite Psalm 84, verses 9–14.

Conclusion: Let us express our deep thanks to God for Christ, the Prince of Peace, by reciting the Gloria of the Mass.

67. THE WISDOM OF CHRIST

Lk. 2, 41–52	Prv. 8, 1–11
Lk. 4, 14–22	8, 12–21
Mt. 7, 24–29	8, 22–31
	8, 32–36

Introduction: In Sacred Scripture God is ever telling us of His Divine Word. In this Scripture reading He communicates to us His teaching on the wisdom of Christ. Let us be attentive as He tells us of the wisdom of the boy Jesus in the Temple of Jerusalem, the wisdom of Jesus as He teaches in the synagogue that He is the Messias, and the astonishment of the people at Jesus' teaching in the Sermon on the Mount. In preparation for our reading let us recite Proverbs 8, verses 1–11.

First Reading: The Word of God as recorded in the Gospel according to St. Luke, chapter 2, verses 41–52. In this reading God is telling us how His Son, Jesus, amazed the teachers at Jerusalem with His wisdom.

℄ In grateful response to the Word we have received, let us recite Proverbs 8, verses 12–21.

Second Reading: The Word of God as recorded in the Gospel according to St. Luke, chapter 4, verses 14–22. In this reading God is telling us of the wisdom of Jesus as He taught the Jews in the synagogue that He is the Messias.

℄ In grateful response to the Word we have received, let us recite Proverbs 8, verses 22–31.

Third Reading: The Word of God as recorded in the Gospel according to St. Matthew, chapter 7, verses 24–29. In this reading God is telling us how astonished the people were at Jesus' beautiful teaching in the Sermon on the Mount.

℄ In grateful response to the Word we have received, let us recite Proverbs 8, verses 32–36.

Conclusion: Let us express our deep thanks to God for Christ's gift of wisdom by reciting this prayer:

O Wisdom, You came forth from the mouth of the Most High, reaching from one end of the heavens to the other and ordering all things mightily and sweetly; come and teach us the way of prudence.

68. THE MERCY OF CHRIST

Mt. 9, 27–31	**Ps.**	**135, 1–9**
Lk. 7, 36–50		**135, 10–16**
Lk. 23, 39–43		**135, 17–22**
		135, 23–26

Introduction: In Sacred Scripture God is ever telling us of His Divine Word. In this Scripture reading He teaches us about the mercy of Christ. Let us be attentive as He tells us of the mercy of Christ in the healing of the two blind men, in the forgiving of the sinful woman, and in the promise to the good thief. In preparation for our reading let us recite Psalm 135, verses 1–9.

First Reading: The Word of God as recorded in the Gospel according to St. Matthew, chapter 9, verses 27–31. In this reading God is telling us that Christ was merciful to the blind.

℄ In grateful response to the Word we have received, let us recite Psalm 135, verses 10–16.

Second Reading: The Word of God as recorded in the Gospel according to St. Luke, chapter 7, verses 36–50. In this reading God is telling us that Christ was merciful to the sinful woman.

℄ In grateful response to the Word we have received, let us recite Psalm 135, verses 17–22.

Third Reading: The Word of God as recorded in the Gospel according to St. Luke, chapter 23, verses 39–43. In this reading God is telling us that in His mercy Christ rewarded the thief on the cross with the promise of Paradise.

℄ In grateful response to the Word we have received, let us recite Psalm 135, verses 23–26.

Conclusion: Let us express our deep thanks to God for the saving mercy of Jesus Christ and let us express our sorrow for sin by reciting an Act of Contrition.

69. CHRIST'S LOVE FOR SINNERS

Lk. 15, 1–7	Pss. 129, 1–8
Lk. 15, 8–10	50, 3–8
Lk. 15, 11–32	50, 9–14
	50, 15–19

Introduction: God our Father speaks to us through His living Word. In this Scripture reading He teaches us about Christ's love for sinners. Let us be attentive as He tells us that Christ's love for sinners is portrayed by three parables: the shepherd going after the wandering sheep; the woman searching for the lost coin; and the father welcoming back his wayward son. In preparation for our reading let us recite Psalm 129, verses 1–8.

First Reading: The Word of God as recorded in the Gospel according to St. Luke, chapter 15, verses 1–7. In this reading God is telling us that the shepherd going after the wandering sheep is Christ going after the wandering sinner.

¶ In grateful response to the Word we have received, let us recite Psalm 50, verses 3–8.

Second Reading: The Word of God as recorded in the Gospel according to St. Luke, chapter 15, verses 8–10. In this reading God is teaching us that the woman searching for the lost coin is Christ searching for the sinner.

¶ In grateful response to the Word we have received, let us recite Psalm 50, verses 9–14.

Third Reading: The Word of God as recorded in the Gospel according to St. Luke, chapter 15, verses 11–32. In this reading God is telling us that the father welcoming back the wayward son with open arms symbolizes Christ welcoming back the sinner who is sorry for his sins.

¶ In grateful response to the Word we have received, let us recite Psalm 50, verses 15–19.

Conclusion: Let us express our deep thanks to God for His loving-kindness to us even when we have sinned by reciting the Confiteor.

70. THE CHARITY OF CHRIST

Jn. 10, 11–18	Pss.	116, 1–2
Jn. 15, 9–17		22, 1–6
Rom. 8, 35–39		35, 6–10
		39, 2–6

Introduction: In Sacred Scripture God is ever telling us of His Divine Word. In this Scripture reading He teaches us about the charity of Christ. Let us be attentive as He tells us that Christ was willing to lay down His life out of love for His followers; that Christ, about to suffer, told of His deep love for His disciples; and that Christ's deep love for us makes us inseparable from Him. In preparation for our reading let us recite Psalm 116, verses 1–2.

First Reading: The Word of God as recorded in the Gospel according to St. John, chapter 10, verses 11–18. In this reading God is telling us that Christ so loved us that He willingly laid down His life for us.

¶ In grateful response to the Word we have received, let us recite Psalm 22, verses 1–6.

Second Reading: The Word of God as recorded in the Gospel according to St. John, chapter 15, verses 9–17. In this reading God is telling us that Christ told His disciples at the Last Supper how much He loved them.

¶ In grateful response to the Word we have received, let us recite Psalm 35, verses 6–10.

Third Reading: The Word of God as recorded in the Epistle to the Romans, chapter 8, verses 35–39. In this reading God is telling us that Christ's love for us is so perfect that no power in heaven or on earth can separate us from Him.

¶ In grateful response to the Word we have received, let us recite Psalm 39, verses 2–6.

Conclusion: Let us show our gratitude to God for teaching us about the infinite love of His Son for us by reciting this prayer:

O Lord Jesus Christ, Good Shepherd, You died freely upon the cross for us, Your people; grant us, we pray, the spirit of love, that as You have loved us we may learn to love one another.

71. THE JUSTICE OF CHRIST

Mt. 22, 15–22	Pss.	42, 1–5
Jn. 5, 22–30		9a, 2–9
Mt. 25, 31–46		81, 1–8
		71, 1–14

Introduction: God, who rewards the just and punishes the evil, speaks to us through His living Word. In this Scripture reading He teaches us about the justice of Christ. Let us be attentive as He tells us of the justice of Christ in rendering to Caesar the things that are Caesar's, and to God the things that are God's; and of the justice of Christ at the Last Judgment, when He shall separate the good from the bad. In preparation for our reading let us recite Psalm 42, verses 1–5.

First Reading: The Word of God as recorded in the Gospel according to St. Matthew, chapter 22, verses 15–22. In this reading God is telling us of the justice of Christ in rendering to Caesar the things that are Caesar's, and to God the things that are God's.

¶ In grateful response to the Word we have received, let us recite Psalm 9a, verses 2–9.

Second Reading: The Word of God as recorded in the Gospel according to St. John, chapter 5, verses 22–30. In this reading God is telling us that the final judgment by the Son of Man, Jesus Christ, will be just.

¶ In grateful response to the Word we have received, let us recite Psalm 81, verses 1–8.

Third Reading: The Word of God as recorded in the Gospel according to St. Matthew, chapter 25, verses 31–46. In this reading God is telling us that at the Last Judgment His Son will justly separate the good for heaven and the bad for hell.

℄ In grateful response to the Word we have received, let us recite Psalm 71, verses 1–14.

Conclusion: Let us express our deep thanks to God for our just Judge, Jesus Christ, by reciting this prayer:

O God, You have appointed Your Son, Jesus Christ, the Judge of all men; grant that by our prayer and penance we may repair our sinful lives and be numbered among the elect on Judgment Day.

72. THE PATIENCE OF CHRIST

Is. 53, 3–7	Jb. 16, 7–17
Mt. 26, 47–56	Jb. 16, 18–17, 2
Lk. 23, 33–46	Jb. 30, 9–22
	Jb. 30, 23–31

Introduction: In Sacred Scripture God is ever telling us of His Divine Word. In this Scripture reading He teaches us about the patience of Christ. Let us be attentive as He tells us that the Christ would patiently and silently suffer for our sins, and that He did not turn away from those who persecuted Him but asked God to forgive them. In preparation for our reading let us recite Job 16, verses 7–17.

First Reading: The Word of God as recorded in the Book of Isaias, chapter 53, verses 3–7. In this reading God is telling us that according to prophecy the Christ would patiently and silently take on our infirmities and sorrows.

℄ In grateful response to the Word we have received, let us recite Job 16, verse 18 to chapter 17, verse 2.

Second Reading: The Word of God as recorded in the Gospel according to St. Matthew, chapter 26, verses 47–56. In this reading

God is telling us that in His patience Christ did not turn away from those who persecuted Him.

¶ In grateful response to the Word we have received, let us recite Job 30, verses 9–22.

Third Reading: The Word of God as recorded in the Gospel according to St. Luke, chapter 23, verses 33–46. In this reading God is telling us that Christ on the cross patiently asked God's forgiveness for those who persecuted Him.

¶ In grateful response to the Word we have received, let us recite Job 30, verses 23–31.

Conclusion: Let us express our deep thanks to God for Christ's example of patience by reciting this prayer:

O God of mercy, You sent Your Son upon earth to be wounded for our iniquities and bruised for our sins; by Your kindness give us, we pray, the light to know our faults and the humility to confess them.

73. THE SUFFERING MESSIAS

Jer. 8, 18–9, 3	Pss.	141, 2–8
Mt. 27, 26–50		68, 17–22
Acts 13, 23–33		101, 2–12
		117, 1–17

Introduction: In Sacred Scripture God is ever telling us of His Divine Word. In this Scripture reading He communicates to us His teaching on the suffering Messias. Let us be attentive as He tells us that the sufferings of Jesus, the Messias, were foreshadowed by the holy prophet Jeremias; that they were endured by our Lord Jesus in His Passion and death on the cross; and that Jesus' sufferings led to His glorious Resurrection. In preparation for our reading let us recite Psalm 141, verses 2–8.

First Reading: The Word of God as recorded in the Book of Jeremias, chapter 8, verse 18 to chapter 9, verse 3. In this reading God is describing the grief of Jeremias, a type of the suffering Christ.

℄ In response to the Word we have received, let us recite with Christ Psalm 68, verses 17–22.

Second Reading: The Word of God as recorded in the Gospel according to St. Matthew, chapter 27, verses 26–50. In this reading God is telling us of the sufferings which Jesus endured for us in His Passion and death on the cross.

℄ In response to the Word we have received let us join with Christ in His sufferings and recite Psalm 101, verses 2–12.

Third Reading: The Word of God as recorded in the Acts of the Apostles, chapter 13, verses 23–33. In this reading God is telling us through St. Paul that the sufferings and death of Jesus led to His glorious Resurrection.

℄ In joyful response to the Word we have received, let us recite with Christ who has suffered and died and risen for us Psalm 117, verses 1–17.

Conclusion: Let us ask God to bless us through the sufferings of His Son by reciting this prayer:

Look down, O Lord, on this Your family and bless us, we pray, for whom our Lord Jesus Christ willingly gave Himself into the hands of wicked men and suffered the torments of the cross.

74. JESUS LIFTED UP ON THE CROSS

Nm. 21, 4–9	Pss.	21, 2–6
Jn. 3, 10–17		17, 2–7
Jn. 19, 15–30		122, 1–4
Phil. 2, 5–11		21, 15–20
		8, 2–10

Introduction: God our Father speaks to us through His living Word. In this Scripture reading He communicates to us His teaching on Jesus lifted up on the cross. Let us be attentive as He tells us that the lifting up of Jesus on the cross was foreshadowed by the brazen serpent, was accomplished on Calvary, and was preached by St. Paul. In preparation for our reading let us recite Psalm 21, verses 2–6.

First Reading: The Word of God as recorded in the Book of Numbers, chapter 21, verses 4–9. In this reading God is telling us that He saved His people in the desert by having Moses lift up the brazen serpent.

℄ In grateful response to the Word we have received, let us recite **Psalm 17, verses 2–7.**

Second Reading: The Word of God as recorded in the Gospel according to St. John, chapter 3, verses 10–17. In this reading God is telling us that Jesus spoke of Himself as being lifted up as the serpent was in the desert.

℄ In grateful response to the Word we have received, let us recite Psalm 122, verses 1–4.

Third Reading: The Word of God as recorded in the Gospel according to St. John, chapter 19, verses 15–30. In this reading God is telling us that Jesus fulfilled what was foreshadowed by the brazen serpent when He was lifted up on the cross.

℄ In grateful response to the Word we have received, let us recite Psalm 21, verses 15–20.

Fourth Reading: The Word of God as recorded in the Epistle to the Philippians, chapter 2, verses 5–11. In this reading God is telling us through St. Paul that, because Jesus was lifted up on the cross, God has lifted Him up to heaven.

℄ In grateful response to the Word we have received, let us recite Psalm 8, verses 2–10.

Conclusion: Let us express our deep thanks to God for the lifting up of Jesus, both on the cross and to heaven, by reciting "The Prayer to Jesus Crucified":

Behold, O kind and most sweet Jesus, I cast myself upon my knees in Your sight, and, with the most fervent desire of my soul, I pray and beg You to impress upon my heart lively sentiments of faith, hope, and charity, with true contrition for my sins and a firm purpose of amendment; while with deep affection and grief of soul I ponder within myself and mentally contemplate Your five wounds, having before my eyes the words which David the prophet put on Your lips concerning You: "They have pierced my hands and my feet; I can count all my bones."

75. THE RESURRECTION OF CHRIST

Jon. 1,	1–2,	1 & 11	Ps.	15,	7–11
Mt. 12,	38–40		Jon.	2,	2–10
Lk. 24,	1–8		Pss.	117,	19–25
				97,	1–9

Introduction: In the Sacred Scripture God is ever telling us of His Divine Word. In this Scripture reading He communicates to us His teaching on the Resurrection of Christ. Let us be attentive as He tells us that Jonas was swallowed by a giant fish but after three days was miraculously cast up alive on land; and that Jesus used this story to point to His own burial and Resurrection on the third day. In preparation for our reading let us recite Psalm 15, verses 7–11.

First Reading: The Word of God as recorded in the Book of Jonas, chapter 1, verse 1 to chapter 2, verses 1 and 11. In this reading God is telling us the story of Jonas who was cast up alive after three days inside a giant fish.

℄ In grateful response to the Word we have received, let us recite Jonas 2, verses 2–10.

Second Reading: The Word of God as recorded in the Gospel according to St. Matthew, chapter 12, verses 38–40. In this reading God is telling us of Jesus' prophecy that, like Jonas, He would come forth alive from His tomb on the third day.

℄ In grateful response to the Word we have received, let us recite Psalm 117, verses 19–25.

Third Reading: The Word of God as recorded in the Gospel according to St. Luke, chapter 24, verses 1–8. In this reading God is telling us that Jesus did what He said He would do: He arose from the tomb on the third day.

℄ In grateful response to the Word we have received, let us recite Psalm 97, verses 1–9.

Conclusion: Let us express our deep thanks to God for the Resurrection of Jesus Christ, our Lord, by reciting this prayer:

All-powerful and ever-living God, grant us, Your faithful, the grace of entering fully into the mysteries of Your Son's Resurrection; that by renewing our baptismal promises we may forever renounce sin and have a fuller share in His victory.

76. THREE APPEARANCES OF JESUS AFTER THE RESURRECTION

Lk. 24, 13–32		Ps.	91,	2–9
Jn. 20, 19–23		Wis.	2,	23–3, 9
Mt. 28, 16–20		Jer.	33,	6–9
		Ps.	150,	1–6

Introduction: In Sacred Scripture God is ever telling us of His Divine Word. In this Scripture reading He describes for us the appearances of Jesus after the Resurrection. Let us be attentive as He tells us that Christ manifested Himself as the risen Lord to the disciples at Emmaus; He appeared to the apostles in the upper room giving them the power to forgive sin; and He appeared again before His glorious Ascension into heaven, commanding them to go forth and make disciples of all nations. In preparation for our reading let us recite Psalm 91, verses 2–9.

First Reading: The Word of God as recorded in the Gospel according to St. Luke, chapter 24, verses 13–32. In this reading God is telling us that Christ manifested Himself as the risen Lord to the disciples at Emmaus.
¶ In grateful response to the Word we have received, let us recite Wisdom 2, verse 23 to chapter 3, verse 9.

Second Reading: The Word of God as recorded in the Gospel according to St. John, chapter 20, verses 19–23. In this reading God is telling us that Christ appeared to the apostles in the upper room and gave them the power to forgive sin.
¶ In grateful response to the Word we have received, let us recite Jeremias 33, verses 6–9.

Third Reading: The Word of God as recorded in the Gospel according to St. Matthew, chapter 28, verses 16–20. In this reading God is telling us that Jesus appeared again before His glorious

Ascension into heaven, commanding the apostles to go forth and make disciples of all nations.

ℭ In grateful response to the Word we have received, let us recite Psalm 150, verses 1–6.

Conclusion: Let us express our deep thanks to God for the apparitions of Christ after the Resurrection by reciting the Our Father.

77. THE ASCENSION OF JESUS INTO HEAVEN

Lk. 19, 12–28	Pss.	46, 2–10
Acts 1, 1–11		67, 2–7
Heb. 9, 24–28		67, 16–21
		98, 1–9

Introduction: God our Father instructs us through His living Word. In this Scripture reading He communicates to us His teaching on the Ascension of Jesus into heaven. Let us be attentive as He tells us that the Ascension of Jesus was hinted at by the parable of the nobleman; actually took place after the Resurrection in the presence of the apostles; and is the pledge that the Christ, who now reigns in heaven, will return to judge and save us at His Second Coming. In preparation for our reading let us recite Psalm 46, verses 2–10.

First Reading: The Word of God as recorded in the Gospel according to St. Luke, chapter 19, verses 12–28. In this reading God is telling us how Jesus hinted at His own Ascension when He told the parable of the nobleman who went on a long journey in order to receive a kingdom.

ℭ In grateful response to the Word we have received, let us recite Psalm 67, verses 2–7.

Second Reading: The Word of God as recorded in the Acts of the Apostles, chapter 1, verses 1–11. In this reading God is telling us that Christ, the king of all noblemen, ascended into heaven in the presence of His apostles.

ℭ In grateful response to the Word we have received, let us recite Psalm 67, verses 16–21.

Third Reading: The Word of God as recorded in the Epistle to the Hebrews, chapter 9, verses 24–28. In this reading God is telling us that Jesus is in heaven and will return to judge and save us at His Second Coming.

¶ In grateful response to the Word we have received, let us recite Psalm 98, verses 1–9.

Conclusion: Let us express our deep thanks to God for the Ascension of Jesus into heaven by reciting this prayer:

O Lord, King of Glory, by Your Ascension You fulfilled the prophecies, returned to Your Father's house, and opened the gates of heaven to man; give us, we pray, a full share in Your Redemption, so that when You return as our Judge we may ascend with You to the throne of God.

78. ANOINTING BY THE SPIRIT OF GOD

1 Sm. (1 Kgs.)	16,	1–13	Is.	11,	1–3a
Lk.	4,	14–22	Pss.	131,	11–18
Acts	2,	1–11		44,	2–8
				103,	30–35

Introduction: God our Father speaks to us through His living Word. In this Scripture reading He gives us His teaching on anointing by the Spirit of God. Let us be attentive as He tells us of the anointing of David, king of Israel; of the coming of Christ our messianic King, anointed with the Holy Spirit; and of the anointing of Christ's Church at Pentecost by the same Holy Spirit. In preparation for our reading let us recite Isaias 11, verses 1–3a.

First Reading: The Word of God as recorded in the First Book of Samuel, chapter 16, verses 1–13. In this reading God is telling us that David was anointed king of Israel and that the Spirit of the Lord came upon him.

¶ In grateful response to the Word we have received, let us recite Psalm 131, verses 11–18.

Second Reading: The Word of God as recorded in the Gospel according to St. Luke, chapter 4, verses 14–22. In this reading God is telling us that Jesus Christ is the Anointed One who fulfills the hopes of the Old Testament.

¶ In grateful response to the Word we have received, let us recite Psalm 44, verses 2–8.

Third Reading: The Word of God as recorded in the Acts of the Apostles, chapter 2, verses 1–11. In this reading God is telling us that the Church is anointed with the Holy Spirit at Pentecost to continue the work of Christ.

¶ In grateful response to the Word we have received, let us recite Psalm 103, verses 30–35.

Conclusion: Let us express our deep thanks to God for having sent His anointing Spirit upon David, upon Christ, and upon His Church by reciting this prayer:

O God, You taught the faithful by sending the light of the Holy Spirit into their hearts; grant that, by the gift of the same Spirit, right judgment may be ours, and we may ever find joy in His comfort.

79. THE CHURCH AS ONE

Ez.	37, 15–28		Mi.	4, 1–4
Jn.	17, 20–26		Pss.	121, 1–9
1 Cor.	12, 12–20			22, 1–6
				132, 1–3

Introduction: The Holy Spirit, who has entrusted His living Word to the Church, speaks to us. In this Scripture reading He communicates to us His teaching on the Church as one. Let us be attentive as He tells us that He promised His Church would be one; that Christ's last prayer before He died was that the Church would be one; and that the Mystical Body of Christ, the Church, is one. In preparation for our reading let us recite Micheas 4, verses 1–4.

First Reading: The Word of God as recorded in the Book of Ezechiel, chapter 37, verses 15–28. In this reading God is telling us in the allegory of the two sticks of His promise that His Church, the new Israel, would be one.

¶ In grateful response to the Word we have received, let us recite Psalm 121, verses 1–9.

Second Reading: The Word of God as recorded in the Gospel according to St. John, chapter 17, verses 20–26. In this reading God is telling us that Christ's last prayer before He died was that the Church would be one.

¶ In grateful response to the Word we have received, let us recite Psalm 22, verses 1–6.

Third Reading: The Word of God as recorded in the First Epistle to the Corinthians, chapter 12, verses 12–20. In this reading God is telling us, through St. Paul, that the Mystical Body of Christ, the Church, is one.

¶ In grateful response to the Word we have received, let us recite Psalm 132, verses 1–3.

Conclusion: Let us express our deep thanks to God for His teaching and let us pray for the unity of the Church:

O God, You correct those who are in error, You gather those who are separated, You are the guardian of Your Flock; pour down upon Christian people, we pray, the Spirit of unity, that putting aside all divisions they may give themselves entirely to the true Shepherd of Your Church and be able to serve You worthily.

80. THE CHURCH AS HOLY

Ex.	19, 1–8		Pss.	23,	1–10
Jn.	17, 9–19			106,	1–9
1 Pt.	2, 1–10		Is.	4,	2–6
			Jl.	3,	17–21

Introduction: The Holy Spirit, who has entrusted His living Word to the Church, speaks to us. In this Scripture reading He teaches us that the Church is holy. Let us be attentive as He tells us that He called the Israel of old to be His Holy Nation; that Jesus prayed that the Church, the New Israel, might be a Holy Nation; and that the Church truly is a Holy Nation. In preparation for our reading let us recite Psalm 23, verses 1–10.

First Reading: The Word of God as recorded in the Book of Exodus, chapter 19, verses 1–8. In this reading God is telling us that He, through His prophet Moses, called Israel to be His People, a Holy Nation.

℄ In grateful response to the Word we have received, let us recite Psalm 106, verses 1–9.

Second Reading: The Word of God as recorded in the Gospel according to St. John, chapter 17, verses 9–19. In this reading God is telling us that Jesus, the New Moses, prayed that the Church, the New Israel, would be "sanctified in truth," that it might be a Holy Nation.

℄ In grateful response to the Word we have received, let us recite Isaias 4, verses 2–6.

Third Reading: The Word of God as recorded in the First Epistle of St. Peter, chapter 2, verses 1–10. In this reading God is telling us that the Church, His new People, is a Chosen Race, a Holy Nation.

℄ In grateful response to the Word we have received, let us recite Joel 3, verses 17–21.

Conclusion: Let us express our deep thanks to God for the Church, His Holy Nation, by reciting this prayer:

O Lord God, Your Son at the Last Supper prayed that the Church would be sanctified in truth; send us, we ask of You, the Spirit of holiness, that we, Your servants, may be a Chosen Race, a Royal Priesthood, a Holy Nation, a Purchased People.

81. THE CHURCH AS CATHOLIC

Is. 2, 1–4	Pss.	46, 2–10
Mk. 11, 15–17		86, 1–7
Mt. 28, 16–20		71, 8–11
Acts 13, 44–49		116, 1–2
		66, 2–8

Introduction: The Holy Spirit, who has entrusted His living Word to the Church, speaks to us. In this Scripture reading He teaches us about the Church as catholic. Let us be attentive as He tells us that a universal or catholic Church was foretold by the prophet

Isaias; was prepared for by Christ during His ministry, and was finally established as such upon the apostles when Christ sent them forth as messengers of the Gospel to the Gentiles. In preparation for our reading let us recite Psalm 46, verses 2–10.

First Reading: The Word of God as recorded in the Book of Isaias, chapter 2, verses 1–4. In this reading God is telling us that many people from all nations will come and join His Church.

¶ In grateful response to the Word we have received, let us recite Psalm 86, verses 1–7.

Second Reading: The Word of God as recorded in the Gospel according to St. Mark, chapter 11, verses 15–17. In this reading God is telling us that Christ cleansed the Temple, making it a House of Prayer for all men.

¶ In grateful response to the Word we have received, let us recite Psalm 71, verses 8–11.

Third Reading: The Word of God as recorded in the Gospel according to St. Matthew, chapter 28, verses 16–20. In this reading God is telling us that Christ commanded that all nations be baptized and made members of His Church.

¶ In grateful response to the Word we have received, let us recite Psalm 116, verses 1–2.

Fourth Reading: The Word of God as recorded in the Acts of the Apostles, chapter 13, verses 44–49. In this reading God is telling us that His apostles, messengers of the Gospel, are to be means of salvation to every nation on earth.

¶ In grateful response to the Word we have received, let us recite Psalm 66, verses 2–8.

Conclusion: Let us express our deep thanks to God for the Catholic Church and pray for the propagation of the faith:

O God, it is Your desire that all men be saved and come to the knowledge of the truth; send forth, we pray, laborers to the harvest of souls, and give them strength to proclaim Your Word with all confidence; that Your Good News may be known and loved everywhere and that all nations may adore You, the one true God, together with Your Son, Jesus Christ, our Lord, whom You have sent.

82. THE CHURCH AS APOSTOLIC

Mk.	3, 13–19		Sir.	44, 1–15
Lk.	22, 24–30		Pss.	14, 1–5
Eph.	2, 17–22			83, 2–13
				101, 13–19

Introduction: The Holy Spirit, who has entrusted His living Word to the Church, speaks to us. In this Scripture reading He teaches us about the Church as apostolic. Let us be attentive as He tells us that Christ chose twelve apostles as leaders of His Church; that He gave them power to rule over His Church; and that His Church is built on the firm foundation of the apostles. In preparation for our reading let us recite Sirach 44, verses 1–15.

First Reading: The Word of God as recorded in the Gospel according to St. Mark, chapter 3, verses 13–19. In this reading God is telling us that He chose the apostles as teachers and first members of His Church.

℄ In grateful response to the Word we have received, let us recite Psalm 14, verses 1–5.

Second Reading: The Word of God as recorded in the Gospel according to St. Luke, chapter 22, verses 24–30. In this reading God is telling us that the apostles are to rule over His Church.

℄ In grateful response to the Word we have received, let us recite Psalm 83, verses 2–13.

Third Reading: The Word of God as recorded in the Epistle to the Ephesians, chapter 2, verses 17–22. In this reading God is telling us that His Church is built upon the firm foundation of the apostles.

℄ In grateful response to the Word we have received, let us recite Psalm 101, verses 13–19.

Conclusion: Let us express our deep thanks to God for the Apostolic Church by reciting this prayer:

Graciously receive the prayers of Your Church, we beg You, Lord; so that built upon the firm foundation of the apostles she may ever triumph over opposition and error, and serve You in safety and freedom.

83. THE CHURCH COMPOSED OF THE POOR AND HUMBLE

Lk. 14, 12–15		Mi.	4, 6–8
Lk. 14, 15–24		Pss.	144, 14–21
Lk. 1, 39–55			69, 2–6
			145, 1–10

Introduction: God our Father speaks to us through His living Word. In this Scripture reading He communicates to us His teaching on the Church composed of the poor and humble. Let us be attentive as He tells us in two parables that His Church is composed of the poor, the humble, the crippled, the blind, and the lame; and that this ideal of the humble member of Christ's Church has no better example than the Virgin Mother of God. In preparation for our reading let us recite Micheas 4, verses 6–8.

First Reading: The Word of God as recorded in the Gospel according to St. Luke, chapter 14, verses 12–15. In this reading God is telling us that His kingdom, the Church, is composed of the poor, the blind, and the lame.

℄ In grateful response to the Word we have received, let us recite Psalm 144, verses 14–21.

Second Reading: The Word of God as recorded in the Gospel according to St. Luke, chapter 14, verses 15–24. In this reading God is telling us again that it is the poor, the blind, the lame, and the sick who shall eat at the messianic banquet of His Church.

℄ In grateful response to the Word we have received, let us recite Psalm 69, verses 2–6.

Third Reading: The Word of God as recorded in the Gospel according to St. Luke, chapter 1, verses 39–55. In this reading God is showing us the ideal, humble member of Christ's Church: the Virgin Mother of God.

℄ In grateful response to the Word we have received, let us recite Psalm 145, verses 1–10.

Conclusion: Let us express our deep thanks to God for making us, His poor and humble servants, members of His Church by reciting the Beatitudes in the Gospel according to St. Matthew, chapter 5, verses 3–12.

84. THE CHURCH AS THE NEW JERUSALEM

2 Sm. (2 Kgs.)	6, 1–18	Pss.	146, 1–5
Lk.	2, 40–50		131, 1–10
Ap.	21, 1–4		131, 11–18
		Za.	8, 3–8

Introduction: The Holy Spirit, who has entrusted His living Word to the Church, speaks to us. In this Scripture reading He teaches us about the Church, the New Jerusalem. Let us be attentive as He tells us that in the Old Testament David brought the Ark of the Covenant, God's dwelling place, to Jerusalem; that in the New Testament Christ must dwell in Jerusalem, the city of His Father; and that the Church, the New Jerusalem, will be complete when God dwells among His People in the Heavenly City. In preparation for our reading let us recite Psalm 146, verses 1–5.

First Reading: The Word of God as recorded in the Second Book of Samuel, chapter 6, verses 1–18. In this reading God is telling us that David brought the Ark of the Covenant to Jerusalem, prefiguring God's dwelling in the Jerusalem of the New Testament, the Church.

¶ In grateful response to the Word we have received, let us recite Psalm 131, verses 1–10.

Second Reading: The Word of God as recorded in the Gospel according to St. Luke, chapter 2, verses 40–50. In this reading God is telling us that His Son, Jesus Christ, must dwell in Jerusalem, the dwelling place of the Father: "Did you not know that I must be in My Father's House?"

¶ In grateful response to the Word we have received, let us recite Psalm 131, verses 11–18.

Third Reading: The Word of God as recorded in the Apocalypse, chapter 21, verses 1–4. In this reading God is telling us that He will dwell among His people in the New and Heavenly Jerusalem, the fulfillment of His Church.

¶ In grateful response to the Word we have received, let us recite Zacharias 8, verses 3–8.

Conclusion: Let us express our deep thanks to God for the Church, the New Jerusalem, by reciting this prayer:

Shower Your loving-kindness upon us, Your People, O Lord; and assure us who are members of Your Church on earth a place in the Heavenly Jerusalem.

85. THE CHURCH AS THE MYSTICAL BODY OF CHRIST

1 Cor.	12,	12–31	Pss.	147,	12–20
Eph.	4,	1–16		132,	1–3
1 Cor.	6,	12–20		126,	1–5
				143,	9–15

Introduction: The Holy Spirit, who has entrusted His living Word to the Church, speaks to us. In this Scripture reading He teaches us about the Church as the Mystical Body of Christ. Let us be attentive as He tells us that the members of the Church are all united in one Body, of which Christ is the Head; and that we should keep our lives pure, because we are members of Christ's Body. In preparation for our reading let us recite Psalm 147, verses 12–20.

First Reading: The Word of God as recorded in the First Epistle to the Corinthians, chapter 12, verses 12–31. In this reading God is telling us that the members of the Church are united with one another as members of a body.

ℭ In grateful response to the Word we have received, let us recite Psalm 132, verses 1–3.

Second Reading: The Word of God as recorded in the Epistle to the Ephesians, chapter 4, verses 1–16. In this reading God is telling us that the Mystical Body of Christ, the Church, derives its unity from Christ, the Head.

ℭ In grateful response to the Word we have received, let us recite Psalm 126, verses 1–5.

Third Reading: The Word of God as recorded in the First Epistle to the Corinthians, chapter 6, verses 12–20. In this reading God is telling us that one of the great motives to keep our lives pure is that we are members of Christ's Body.

¶ In grateful response to the Word we have received, let us recite Psalm 143, verses 9–15.

Conclusion: Let us express our thanks to Christ, the Head of the Mystical Body, for this instruction; and let us pray for the members of the Church:

O God, all-powerful and eternal, by Your Spirit the whole Body of the Church is made holy and governed; hear our prayers, we beg You, for all ranks of the Church, that by the gift of Your grace, all the members of this Body may pay You loyal service.

86. THE CHURCH, THE ARK OF SALVATION

Gn.	7, 11–24		**Ps.**	**92,**	**1–5**
Ex.	2, 1–10		**Is.**	**54,**	**7–10**
Mk.	4, 35–40		**Pss.**	**39,**	**2–6**
				106,	**23–32**

Introduction: The Holy Spirit, who has entrusted His living Word to the Church, speaks to us. In this Scripture reading He teaches us about the Church as the Ark of Salvation. Let us be attentive as He tells us that the saving power of the Church was foreshadowed: first by Noe's Ark, secondly by the basket in which the child Moses was placed, and thirdly by the boat of the apostles on the Sea of Galilee. In preparation for our reading let us recite Psalm 92, verses 1–5.

First Reading: The Word of God as recorded in the Book of Genesis, chapter 7, verses 11–24. In this reading God is telling us that He miraculously saved the Ark of Noe in the great Flood. The Ark prefigured His saving Church.

¶ In grateful response to the Word we have received, let us recite Isaias 54, verses 7–10.

Second Reading: The Word of God as recorded in the Book of Exodus, chapter 2, verses 1–10. In this reading God is telling us that He protected the child Moses in a basket on the river. This also reminds us of His saving Church.

¶ In grateful response to the Word we have received, let us recite Psalm 39, verses 2–6.

Third Reading: The Word of God as recorded in the Gospel according to St. Mark, chapter 4, verses 35–40. In this reading God is telling us that Jesus calmed the storm on the Sea of Galilee and saved the boat of the apostles, symbolizing the salvation His Church brings.

℄ In grateful response to the Word we have received, let us recite Psalm 106, verses 23–32.

Conclusion: Let us express our deep thanks to God for the Church, our Ark of Salvation, by reciting this prayer:

May Your lasting mercy, O Lord, direct and defend Your Church; and, since You have always rescued her in times when storms raged about, may she now benefit by Your protection and guidance.

87. THE CHURCH AS THE BRIDE OF CHRIST

Dt. 4, 32–40	Ps. 44, 11–18
Mt. 22, 1–14	Ct. 2, 8–14
Ap. 19, 6–9	Ct. 2, 1–7
	Os. 2, 19–23

Introduction: The Holy Spirit, who has entrusted His Word to the Church, speaks to us. In this Scripture reading He teaches us about the Church as the Bride of Christ. Let us be attentive as He tells us that Christ's love for the Church was foreshadowed by the love of God for Israel; was described by Christ Himself in the parable of the marriage feast; and will be fulfilled in heaven at the wedding feast of the Lamb and His Bride, the Church. In preparation for our reading let us recite Psalm 44, verses 11–18.

First Reading: The Word of God as recorded in the Book of Deuteronomy, chapter 4, verses 32–40. In this reading God is telling us how much He loved the Israel of old; this love foreshadowed Christ's love for the new Israel, the Church.

℄ In grateful response to the Word we have received, let us recite Canticle of Canticles 2, verses 8–14.

Second Reading: The Word of God as recorded in the Gospel according to St. Matthew, chapter 22, verses 1–14. In this reading God is telling us that many refuse the invitation to the wedding feast celebrating the marriage of Christ to His Church.

℄ In response to the Word we have received, let us recite Canticle of Canticles 2, verses 1–7.

Third Reading: The Word of God as recorded in the Apocalypse, chapter 19, verses 6–9. In this reading God is telling us that the union of love between Christ and His Church will be celebrated eternally in heaven.

℄ In grateful response to the Word we have received, let us recite Osee 2, verses 19–23.

Conclusion: Let us express our deep thanks to God for the Church, the Bride of Christ, by reciting this prayer:

O, Lord, You have described Your love for Your Church as that of a bridegroom for his bride; grant that we, Your people, may be ever faithful to this most holy union.

88. THE CHURCH AS THE NEW KINGDOM

1 Sm. (1 Kgs.)	10, 17–25	Ps.	94, 1–7
Mk.	4, 26–34	Am.	9, 8–12
Jn.	19, 33–37	Pss.	77, 1–7
			95, 1–13

Introduction: The Holy Spirit, who has entrusted His living Word to the Church, speaks to us. In this Scripture reading He communicates to us His teaching on the Church as the New Kingdom. Let us be attentive as He tells us that the Church as a kingdom was foreshadowed by the formation of Israel into a kingdom; was described by Jesus in parables; and was fulfilled and founded by Jesus, an eternal kingdom, not of this world. In preparation for our reading let us recite Psalm 94, verses 1–7.

First Reading: The Word of God as recorded in the First Book of Samuel, chapter 10, verses 17–25. In this reading God is telling us that He formed Israel into a kingdom when He had Samuel anoint Saul as its first king. This foreshadowed the Church as a kingdom.

¶ In grateful response to the Word we have received, let us recite Amos 9, verses 8–12.

Second Reading: The Word of God as recorded in the Gospel according to St. Mark, chapter 4, verses 26–34. In this reading God is telling us that Jesus described His Church when He spoke of the kingdom of God in parables.
¶ In grateful response to the Word we have received, let us recite Psalm 77, verses 1–7.

Third Reading: The Word of God as recorded in the Gospel according to St. John, chapter 18, verses 33–37. In this reading God is telling us that His new kingdom is an eternal kingdom, not of this world.
¶ In grateful response to the Word we have received, let us recite Psalm 95, verses 1–13.

Conclusion: Let us express our deep thanks to God for His New Kingdom, the Church, by reciting the Our Father.

89. THE CHURCH AS A VINEYARD

Is. 5, 1–7		Is. 27, 2–6
Lk. 20, 9–19		Pss. 79, 9–16
Jn. 15, 1–11		117, 22–29
		Sir. 24, 17–21 (Douay, 23–31)

Introduction: The Holy Spirit, who has entrusted His living Word to the Church, speaks to us. In this Scripture reading He teaches us about the Church as a vineyard. Let us be attentive as He tells us that Israel of old was like a vineyard which first rejected God and then His beloved Son; and that the New Israel, the Church, is also like a vineyard in which Christ is the vine, the Father is the vinedresser, and we are the branches. In preparation for our reading let us recite Isaias 27, verses 2–6.

First Reading: The Word of God as recorded in the Book of Isaias, chapter 5, verses 1–7. In this reading God is telling us that He planted Israel as a vineyard, but His people did not bear fruit.

In response to the Word we have received, let us recite Psalm 79, verses 9–16.

Second Reading: The Word of God as recorded in the Gospel according to St. Luke, chapter 20, verses 9–19. In this reading God is telling us in a parable that Israel is like a vineyard whose wicked vinedressers rejected and killed His own Son.

In response to the Word we have received, let us recite Psalm 117, verses 22–29.

Third Reading: The Word of God as recorded in the Gospel according to St. John, chapter 15, verses 1–11. In this reading God is telling us that the Church, the New Israel, is like a vineyard: Christ is the vine, His Father is the vinedresser, and we are the branches.

In grateful response to the Word we have received, let us recite Sirach 24, verses 17–21.

Conclusion: Let us express our thanks to God for our union with Christ in the Church by reciting this prayer:

O God of Israel, You planted a vineyard and it brought forth wild grapes; grant us, the New Israel, Your Church, that by our union with Christ, the true vine, we may be cleansed of our sins and bear much fruit.

90. THE CHURCH, THE TEMPLE OF GOD

3 Kgs. 8, 1–13	Pss. 91, 13–16
Ag. 2, 1–10	131, 7–14
Eph. 2, 13–22	Za. 1, 16–17
	Ps. 83, 2–13

Introduction: The Holy Spirit, who has entrusted His living Word to the Church, speaks to us. In this Scripture reading He communicates to us His teaching on the Church, the Temple of God. Let us be attentive as He tells us that the Church was foreshadowed by the Temple built by Solomon; that through His prophet He promised a new Temple, greater than the first; and that this new Temple, the Church, was founded by His Son Jesus. In preparation for our reading let us recite Psalm 91, verses 13–16.

First Reading: The Word of God as recorded in the Third Book of Kings, chapter 8, verses 1–13. In this reading God is telling us that He dwelt in the Temple built by Solomon. This temple foreshadowed the Temple that Christ was to build.

℄ In grateful response to the Word we have received, let us recite Psalm 131, verses 7–14.

Second Reading: The Word of God as recorded in the Book of Aggeus, chapter 2, verses 1–10. In this reading God is telling us that He promised the new Temple, the Church, which was to be greater than the first.

℄ In grateful response to the Word we have received, let us recite Zacharias 1, verses 16–17.

Third Reading: The Word of God as recorded in the Epistle to the Ephesians, chapter 2, verses 13–22. In this reading God is telling us that His new Temple, the Church, was founded by His Son Jesus.

℄ In grateful response to the Word we have received, let us recite Psalm 83, verses 2–13.

Conclusion: Let us express our deep thanks to God for the Church, the new Temple of God, by reciting this prayer:

O Lord Jesus Christ, the desired of all nations, how lovely is Your dwelling place, the Church!; give to Your People, we pray, the desire to dwell forever in Your House and the grace to remain in it.

91. BAPTISM

Ex.	14,	23–31	Ps.	41,	2–6
Jn.	3,	1–8	Ex.	15,	1–13
1 Cor.	10,	1–11	Is.	44,	1–8
			Lk.	1,	68–79

Introduction: God our Father speaks to us through His living Word. In this Scripture reading He communicates to us His teaching on baptism. Let us be attentive as He tells us that He foreshadowed baptism by saying His Chosen People in the waters of the Red Sea; that to become a member of the new Chosen People — the

Church — one must be reborn in the waters of baptism; and that since we are the new Chosen People we must pray that we do not lose the friendship of God gained by baptism. In preparation for our reading let us recite Psalm 41, verses 2–6.

First Reading: The Word of God as recorded in the Book of Exodus, chapter 14, verses 23–31. In this reading God is telling us how He divided the waters of the Red Sea so that His Chosen People could run through safely and escape their enemies.

℄ In grateful response to the Word we have received, let us recite the Canticle of Moses from the Book of Exodus, chapter 15, verses 1–13.

Second Reading: The Word of God is recorded in the Gospel according to St. John, chapter 3, verses 1–8. In this reading God is telling us that to become a member of the new Chosen People and a citizen of the kingdom of God, one must be reborn through baptism.

℄ In grateful response to the Word we have received, let us recite Isaias 44, verses 1–8.

Third Reading: The Word of God as recorded in the First Epistle to the Corinthians, chapter 10, verses 1–11. In this reading God is telling us that baptism is the beginning of the Christian life. We must work and pray that we do not sin as did the Chosen People after God saved them in the waters of the Red Sea.

℄ In grateful response to the Word we have received, let us recite the Canticle of Zachary from the Gospel according to St. Luke, chapter 1, verses 68–79.

Conclusion: Let us express our deep thanks to God for baptism and renew the faith of our baptism by reciting the Apostles' Creed.

92. BAPTISM

Mt.	3,	1–6	Jer.	31,	7–9
Jn.	1,	29–34	Pss.	26,	1–6
Acts	8,	26–38		28,	1–11
				117,	19–29

Introduction: God our Father speaks to us through His living Word. In this Scripture reading He communicates to us His teaching on baptism. Let us be attentive as He tells us that John the Baptist prepared men by baptizing with water only; that Christ's baptism is with water and the Holy Spirit; and that Christ continues to baptize through the Church. In preparation for our reading let us recite Jeremias 31, verses 7–9.

First Reading: The Word of God as recorded in the Gospel according to St. Matthew, chapter 3, verses 1–6. In this reading God is telling us that John the Baptist, by baptizing with water, prepared men to understand the sacrament of baptism.

℄ In grateful response to the Word we have received, let us recite Psalm 26, verses 1–6.

Second Reading: The Word of God as recorded in the Gospel according to St. John, chapter 1, verses 29–34. In this reading God is telling us that His Son's baptism is with water and the Holy Spirit.

℄ In grateful response to the Word we have received, let us recite Psalm 28, verses 1–11.

Third Reading: The Word of God as recorded in the Acts of the Apostles, chapter 8, verses 26–38. In this reading God is telling us that, as the minister of the Queen of Ethiopia received baptism from the deacon Philip, so too we have received baptism and believe that Jesus Christ is the Son of God.

℄ In grateful response to the Word we have received, let us recite Psalm 117, verses 19–29.

Conclusion: Let us express our deep thanks to God for the sacrament of baptism and renew the faith of our baptism by reciting the Apostles' Creed.

93. CONFIRMATION

Mt.	3, 13–17		Ps.	142,	7–12
Jn.	15, 26–16, 7		Is.	11,	1–3a
Acts	8, 14–17		Jl.	2,	28–29
			Ps.	138,	1–10

Introduction: God our Father speaks to us through His living Word. In this Scripture reading He teaches us about the sacrament of confirmation. Let us be attentive as He tells us that, as the Holy Spirit descended on Christ at the beginning of His public ministry, so He comes upon the followers of Christ, as Jesus promised, in the sacrament of confirmation. In preparation for our reading let us recite Psalm 142, verses 7–12.

First Reading: The Word of God as recorded in the Gospel according to St. Matthew, chapter 3, verses 13–17. In this reading God is telling us that the Holy Spirit confirmed the ministry of Jesus when He was baptized in the Jordan.

℄ In grateful response to the Word we have received, let us recite Isaias 11, verses 1–3a.

Second Reading: The Word of God as recorded in the Gospel according to St. John, chapter 15, verse 26 to chapter 16, verse 7. In this reading God is telling us that Christ promised the gift of the same Holy Spirit to His Church.

℄ In grateful response to the Word we have received, let us recite Joel 2, verses 28–29.

Third Reading: The Word of God as recorded in the Acts of the Apostles, chapter 8, verses 14–17. In this reading God is telling us that St. Peter and St. John bestowed the Holy Spirit on believers by the sacrament of confirmation.

℄ In grateful response to the Word we have received, let us recite Psalm 138, verses 1–10.

Conclusion: Let us express our deep thanks to God for the gift of the Holy Spirit in confirmation by reciting this prayer:

Almighty and everlasting God, You have graciously brought us, Your servants, to a new life in baptism, and You have sent us the fullness of the Holy Spirit in confirmation; fill us, we pray, with love, strength, apostolic fire and zeal, so we may always work for the spread and perfection of the kingdom of God.

94. CONFIRMATION

Gn.	11,	1–9	Pss.	95,	1–13
Acts	2,	1–11		35,	2–13
Acts	19,	1–7		103,	24–35
				137,	1–8

Introduction: God our Father speaks to us through His living Word. In this Scripture reading He teaches about the sacrament of confirmation. Let us be attentive as He tells us that the confusion and disunity of Babel is dispelled by the wonderful coming of the Holy Spirit to the whole Church at Pentecost and to each individual of the Church in the sacrament of confirmation. In preparation for our reading let us recite Psalm 95, verses 1–13.

First Reading: The Word of God as recorded in the Book of Genesis, chapter 11, verses 1–9. In this reading God is telling us that the confusion and disunity at Babel is an example of man's weakness without God's help.

℄ In response to the Word we have received, let us recite Psalm 35, verses 2–13.

Second Reading: The Word of God as recorded in the Acts of the Apostles, chapter 2, verses 1–11. In this reading God is telling us that at Pentecost the Holy Spirit came down upon the Church and the newly-born Christians proclaimed in one tongue the wonderful works of God.

℄ In grateful response to the Word we have received, let us recite Psalm 103, verses 24–35.

Third Reading: The Word of God as recorded in the Acts of the Apostles, chapter 19, verses 1–7. In this reading God is telling us that St. Paul, by imposing hands, conferred the Holy Spirit on twelve men in the sacrament of confirmation.

◖ In grateful response to the Word we have received, let us recite Psalm 137, verses 1–8.

Conclusion: Let us express our deep thanks to God for the sacrament of confirmation by reciting this prayer:

O God, You taught the faithful by sending the light of the Holy Spirit into their hearts; grant that, by the gift of the same Spirit, right judgment may be ours, and we may ever find joy in His comfort.

95. THE HOLY EUCHARIST

Ex.	16, 1–15		Pss.	99, 1–5
Jn.	6, 1–15			94, 1–7
1 Cor.	11, 23–29			22, 1–6
				110, 1–5

Introduction: God our Father speaks to us through His living Word. In this Scripture reading He communicates to us His teaching on the Eucharist. Let us be attentive as He tells us that the Blessed Sacrament was foreshadowed by the manna in the desert, was promised by Jesus in the multiplication of the loaves, and is a partaking of a more perfect Manna in Holy Communion. In preparation for our reading let us recite Psalm 99, verses 1–5.

First Reading: The Word of God as recorded in the Book of Exodus, chapter 16, verses 1–15. In this reading God is telling us that He miraculously sent food to His Chosen People in the desert.

◖ In grateful response to the Word we have received, let us recite Psalm 94, verses 1–7.

Second Reading: The Word of God as recorded in the Gospel according to St. John, chapter 6, verses 1–15. In this reading God is telling us that Jesus gives food in the desert to the New Israel, the Church.

◖ In grateful response to the Word we have received, let us recite Psalm 22, verses 1–6.

Third Reading: The Word of God as recorded in the First Epistle to the Corinthians, chapter 11, verses 23–29. In this reading God is telling us that we eat Manna and partake in the multiplication of the loaves, whenever we gather together to celebrate the Eucharist.

℄ In grateful response to the Word we have received, let us recite Psalm 110, verses 1–5.

Conclusion: Let us express our deep thanks to God for the Blessed Sacrament by reciting this prayer:

Lord Jesus, in this wonderful sacrament You have left us the memorial of Your Passion; enable us, we pray, to adore Your hidden Body and Blood with such faith that we may always feel in our lives the effects of Your Redemption.

96. THE HOLY EUCHARIST

Ex. 12, 21–28		Pss.	23, 1–10
Lk. 22, 14–20			134, 1–9
Ap. 19, 6–10			115, 1–10
		Sir.	15, 1–6

Introduction: God our Father speaks to us through His living Word. In this Scripture reading He teaches us about the Holy Eucharist. Let us be attentive as He tells us that the Eucharistic meal, prefigured by the Passover meal of the Old Covenant, was instituted at the Last Supper, and prepares us for the banquet which Christ will celebrate with His Church in heaven. In preparation for our reading let us recite Psalm 23, verses 1–10.

First Reading: The Word of God as recorded in the Book of Exodus, chapter 12, verses 21–28. In this reading God is telling us of the Jewish Passover meal of the Old Covenant, which prefigured the Eucharist of the New Covenant.

℄ In grateful response to the Word we have received, let us recite Psalm 134, verses 1–9.

Second Reading: The Word of God as recorded in the Gospel according to St. Luke, chapter 22, verses 14–20. In this reading God is telling us that Jesus fulfilled the Jewish Passover meal when He instituted the Eucharist at the Last Supper.

⸿ In grateful response to the Word we have received, let us recite Psalm 115, verses 1–10.

Third Reading: The Word of God as recorded in the Apocalypse, chapter 19, verses 6–10. In this reading God is telling us of the fulfillment of the Eucharist in the banquet which Christ, the Lamb of God, will celebrate with His Church in heaven.

⸿ In grateful response to the Word we have received, let us recite Sirach 15, verses 1–6.

Conclusion: Let us express our deep thanks to God for the Eucharistic meal by reciting this prayer:

O God, we give You thanks for the marvelous gift of the Holy Eucharist, the sacred banquet in which Christ gives Himself as food. We thank You, too, for teaching us that this sacrament makes Christ's Passion present to us today, fills our souls with grace, and gives us a pledge of eternal glory.

97. THE SACRAMENT OF PENANCE

Os.	14,	2–10	**Jer.**	31,	10–14
Lk.	7,	36–50	**Pss.**	142,	1–12
Mt.	9,	1–8		102,	1–10
				40,	2–14

Introduction: God our Father speaks to us through His living Word. In this Scripture reading He communicates to us His teaching on the sacrament of penance. Let us be attentive as He tells us that, just as Jesus forgave the sins of the penitent woman and of the paralytic, so He has given this power of forgiving sins to His Church. In preparation for our reading let us recite the Canticle of Jeremias from the Book of Jeremias, chapter 31, verses 10–14.

First Reading: The Word of God as recorded in the Book of Osee, chapter 14, verses 2–10. In this Scripture reading God is telling us that He reproaches Israel for its sins and promises His protection and blessing if His People will only ask forgiveness.

⸿ In response to the Word we have received, let us recite Psalm 142, verses 1–12.

Second Reading: The Word of God as recorded in the Gospel according to St. Luke, chapter 7, verses 36–50. In this reading God is telling us that His Son, Jesus, forgave the sins of the penitent woman.

¶ In grateful response to the Word we have received, let us recite Psalm 102, verses 1–10.

Third Reading: The Word of God as recorded in the Gospel according to St. Matthew, chapter 9, verses 1–8. In this reading God is telling us that when Jesus forgave the sins of the paralytic the crowds "glorified God who had given such power *to men.*"

¶ In grateful response to the Word we have received, let us recite Psalm 40, verses 2–14.

Conclusion: Let us express our deep thanks to God for the sacrament of penance and renew our sorrow for the countless sins which have been forgiven in this sacrament by reciting the Act of Contrition.

98. THE SACRAMENT OF PENANCE

Nm. 14, 11–20	Tb.	13, 1–9
Mk. 2, 1–12	Pss.	50, 3–14
Jn. 20, 19–23		129 1–8
		31, 1–5

Introduction: God our Father speaks to us through His living Word. In this Scripture reading He communicates to us His teaching on the sacrament of penance. Let us be attentive as He tells us that, as the Lord God graciously forgave the sins of Israel, so also Jesus forgave sins, and conferred this power upon His apostles and their successors. In preparation for our reading let us recite the Canticle of Tobias from the Book of Tobias, chapter 13, verses 1–9.

First Reading: The Word of God as recorded in the Book of Numbers, chapter 14, verses 11–20. In this reading God is telling us that He forgave the Israelites their sins.

¶ In grateful response to the Word we have received, let us recite Psalm 50, verses 3–14.

Second Reading: The Word of God as recorded in the Gospel according to St. Mark, chapter 2, verses 1–12. In this reading God is telling us that Jesus performed a miracle to show that He has the power to forgive sins.

℄ In grateful response to the Word we have received, let us recite Psalm 129, verses 1–8.

Third Reading: The Word of God as recorded in the Gospel according to St. John, chapter 20, verses 19–23. In this reading God is telling us that Jesus granted the power to forgive sins to His apostles and their successors.

℄ In grateful response to the Word we have received, let us recite Psalm 31, verses 1–5.

Conclusion: Let us express our deep thanks to God for the sacrament of penance and renew our sorrow for the countless sins which have been forgiven in this sacrament by reciting an Act of Contrition.

99. EXTREME UNCTION

Nm.	21, 4–9		Pss.	6,	2–8
Lk.	10, 25–37			29,	2–13
Jas.	5, 13–18			40,	2–4
			Is.	38,	10–20

Introduction: God our Father speaks to us through His living Word. In this Scripture reading He communicates to us His teaching on the sacrament of the anointing of the sick. Let us be attentive as He tells us that the brazen serpent foreshadowed Christ's healing power, that the Good Samaritan is Christ healing us, and that this Holy Anointing makes Christ's healing power present to us today. In preparation for our reading let us recite Psalm 6, verses 2–8.

First Reading: The Word of God as recorded in the Book of Numbers, chapter 21, verses 4–9. In this reading God is telling us that He miraculously healed the Israelites in the desert when they looked upon the brazen serpent.

℄ In grateful response to the Word we have received, let us recite Psalm 29, verses 2–13.

Second Reading: The Word of God as recorded in the Gospel according to St. Luke, chapter 10, verses 25–37. In this reading God is telling us that Jesus is the Good Samaritan who loves us and heals our wounds.

℄ In grateful response to the Word we have received, let us recite Psalm 40, verses 2–4.

Third Reading: The Word of God as recorded in the Epistle of St. James, chapter 5, verses 13–18. In this reading God is telling us that Jesus' healing power is made present to us today through the sacrament of the anointing of the sick.

℄ In grateful response to the Word we have received, let us recite the Canticle of Ezechias from the Book of Isaias, chapter 38, verses 10–20.

Conclusion: Let us express our deep thanks to God for the sacrament of the last anointing, and let us pray for the grace of a happy death:

O God of power and goodness, You have given to men both healthful remedies and the sacraments of eternal life; look kindly upon us, and refresh the souls which You have created; that in the hour of death we may be found worthy of being presented, unstained by sin, to You, our Creator.

100. EXTREME UNCTION

Jer.	30,	12–22	Pss.	101,	1–13
Mt.	8,	5–17		84,	2–8
Mk.	6,	7–13		30,	10–17
				114,	1–9

Introduction: God our Father speaks to us through His living Word. In this Scripture reading He teaches us about extreme unction. Let us be attentive as He tells us that He promised to heal the wounds of Israel, and that He fulfilled His promise by sending the Divine Physician, Jesus Christ, who continues to heal through His ministers in the sacrament of extreme unction. In preparation for our reading let us recite Psalm 101, verses 1–13.

First Reading: The Word of God as recorded in the Book of Jeremias, chapter 30, verses 12–22. In this reading God is telling us that He will cure the wounds that afflict His Chosen People, Israel.

℄ In grateful response to the Word we have received, let us recite Psalm 84, verses 2–8.

Second Reading: The Word of God as recorded in the Gospel according to St. Matthew, chapter 8, verses 5–17. In this reading God is telling us that Christ, the Divine Physician, cured the sick and possessed at Capharnaum.

℄ In grateful response to the Word we have received, let us recite Psalm 30, verses 10–17.

Third Reading: The Word of God as recorded in the Gospel according to St. Mark, chapter 6, verses 7–13. In this reading God is telling us that Jesus sent His apostles on their mission of healing and cleansing, just as our priests today heal and comfort the sick through the sacrament of extreme unction.

℄ In grateful response to the Word we have received, let us recite Psalm 114, verses 1–9.

Conclusion: Let us express our deep thanks to God for extreme unction and recite this prayer:

By this holy anointing and His most loving mercy may the Lord forgive us whatever wrong we have done *by the use of sight*. Amen. [Repeat five more times using these phrases: *by the use of hearing; by the use of the sense of smell; by the use of the sense of taste and power of speech; by the use of the sense of touch; by the use of the power to walk.*]

101. THE PRIESTHOOD

Gn. 8, 18–22		Pss. 15, 1–6
Sir. 45, 6–16 (Douay, 7–20)		17, 14–20
Mk. 15, 22–38		98, 6–9
		83, 2–5

Introduction: God our Father speaks to us through His living Word. In this Scripture reading He communicates to us His teaching on the priesthood. Let us be attentive as He tells us of the three stages of the priesthood in salvation history: the priesthood of the family as represented by Noe; and the priesthood of Aaron for the sacrifices of the Old Law; and the eternal priesthood of Jesus Christ, in which priests of today share. In preparation for our reading let us recite Psalm 15, verses 1–6.

First Reading: The Word of God as recorded in the Book of Genesis, chapter 8, verses 18–22. In this reading God is telling us that Noe offered a pleasing sacrifice to Him to thank Him for saving him from the flood.

℄ In grateful response to the Word we have received, let us recite Psalm 17, verses 14–20.

Second Reading: The Word of God as recorded in the Book of Sirach, chapter 45, verses 6–16. In this reading God is telling us that He chose Aaron and his sons to be the priests of His Chosen People.

℄ In grateful response to the Word we have received, let us recite Psalm 98, verses 6–9.

Third Reading: The Word of God as recorded in the Gospel according to St. Mark, chapter 15, verses 22–38. In this reading God is telling us that His Son, Jesus Christ, the Priest, offered a perfect sacrifice by dying on the cross. By this sacrifice He created a new and eternal priesthood in which priests of today share.

℄ In grateful response to the Word we have received, let us recite Psalm 83, verses 2–5.

Conclusion: Let us express our deep thanks to God for the priesthood of Christ and recite this prayer for priests:

O Lord, You have made Your Son the one, eternal High Priest for the glory of Your majesty and the salvation of the human race; grant that those He has chosen to serve and administer His holy mysteries may be found faithful in fulfilling their ministry.

102. THE PRIESTHOOD

Gn.	14, 18–20	Pss.	110, 1–10
Lk.	22, 14–20		109, 1–4
Heb.	4, 14–5, 10		115, 3–10
		Mal.	1, 11

Introduction: God our Father speaks to us through His living Word. In this Scripture reading He teaches us about the priesthood of the New Testament. Let us be attentive as He tells us that the bread and wine sacrifice of Melchisedech was fulfilled when Jesus instituted the Sacrifice of the New Law, which He continues to offer in heaven. Priests of today share in this priesthood and offer the same sacrifice. In preparation for our reading let us recite Psalm 110, verses 1–10.

First Reading: The Word of God as recorded in the Book of Genesis, chapter 14, verses 18–20. In this reading God is telling us that Melchisedech offered a sacrifice of bread and wine, a type of Jesus Christ and His sacrifice.

℄ In grateful response to the Word we have received, let us recite Psalm 109, verses 1–4.

Second Reading: The Word of God as recorded in the Gospel according to St. Luke, chapter 22, verses 14–20. In this reading God is telling us that Jesus instituted the Sacrifice of the New Law at the Last Supper.

℄ In grateful response to the Word we have received, let us recite Psalm 115, verses 3–10.

Third Reading: The Word of God as recorded in the Epistle to the Hebrews, chapter 4, verse 14 to chapter 5, verse 10. In this reading God is telling us that Jesus, a priest like Melchisedech, continues to offer sacrifice in heaven. In this priesthood our priests of today have a share and offer the same sacrifice.

℄ In grateful response to the Word we have received, let us recite Malachias 1, verse 11.

Conclusion: Let us express our thanks to God for the priesthood by reciting this prayer:

O God, You appointed Your Son, Jesus Christ, to be the eternal

High Priest, to offer gifts and sacrifices for sins; give us, Your Chosen People, we pray, a great love for His Holy Sacrifice and the grace to atone with Him for our faults.

103. MATRIMONY

Gn.	2,	15–24	Prv.	31,	10–14
Mt.	19,	3–9	Prv.	31,	15–23
1 Cor.	7,	1–7	Prv.	31,	24–31
			Sir.	26,	13–18 (Douay, 16–24)

Introduction: God our Father speaks to us through His living Word. In this Scripture reading He teaches us about matrimony. Let us be attentive as He tells us that He formulated the law of matrimony in the Garden of Eden, He reaffirmed it through His Divine Son, and through St. Paul He gives advice to the married. In preparation for our reading let us recite Proverbs 31, verses 10–14.

First Reading: The Word of God as recorded in the Book of Genesis, chapter 2, verses 15–24. In this reading God is telling us that He instituted matrimony in the Garden of Eden when Adam and Eve became "two in one flesh."

☾ In grateful response to the Word we have received, let us recite Proverbs 31, verses 15–23.

Second Reading: The Word of God as recorded in the Gospel according to St. Matthew, chapter 19, verses 3–9. In this reading God is telling us that Christ, His Son, reaffirmed the sacredness of the matrimonial bond.

☾ In grateful response to the Word we have received, let us recite Proverbs 31, verses 24–31.

Third Reading: The Word of God as recorded in the First Epistle to the Corinthians, chapter 7, verses 1–7. In this reading God, through St. Paul, gives advice to the married.

☾ In grateful response to the Word we have received, let us recite Sirach 26, verses 13–18.

Conclusion: Let us express our deep thanks to God for the sacrament of matrimony by reciting this prayer:

Almighty and everlasting God, by Your power You created Adam and Eve, our first parents, and joined them in a holy union; sanctify, we pray, the hearts and bodies of those who are married, and unite them, by the grace of the sacrament of matrimony, in love and loyal affection.

104. MATRIMONY

Tb.	8,	4–10	Pss.	127,	1–6
Jn.	2,	1–11		126,	1–5
Eph.	5,	21–33		44,	2–10
				44,	11–18

Introduction: God our Father speaks to us through His living Word. In this Scripture reading He communicates to us His teaching on matrimony. Let us be attentive as He tells us that the union of husband and wife is a holy union as exemplified by the marriage of Tobias and Sara; that Jesus sanctified matrimony by His presence at the wedding feast of Cana; and that Christian marriage is so sublime and mysterious that it is one of the sacraments of the Church. In preparation for our reading let us recite Psalm 127, verses 1–6.

First Reading: The Word of God as recorded in the Book of Tobias, chapter 8, verses 4–10. In this reading God is telling us that the union of husband and wife is a holy union as exemplified by the marriage of Tobias and Sara.

℄ In grateful response to the Word we have received, let us recite Psalm 126, verses 1–5.

Second Reading: The Word of God as recorded in the Gospel according to St. John, chapter 2, verses 1–11. In this reading God is telling us that Christ sanctified marriage by His presence at the wedding feast of Cana.

℄ In grateful response to the Word we have received, let us recite Psalm 44, verses 2–10.

Third Reading: The Word of God as recorded in the Epistle to the Ephesians, chapter 5, verses 21–33. In this reading God is telling us that the union of Christian marriage is so sublime and mysterious that it can be compared to the love of Christ for His Bride, the Church. It is a sacrament of the Church.

¶ In grateful response to the Word we have received, let us recite Psalm 44, verses 11–18.

Conclusion: Let us express our deep thanks to God for giving to us through His Word a deeper and richer insight into the meaning of matrimony by reciting this prayer:

Lord Jesus Christ, You loved the Church and delivered Yourself up for her; grant that our married couples, in imitation of You, may live together in a spirit of self-sacrificing love.

105. MARY, THE DAUGHTER OF SION

So. 3, 14–20	Prv. 8, 22–31
Za. 2, 10–13	Mi. 4, 6–10
Lk. 1, 26–38	Pss. 131, 11–18
	86, 1–7

Introduction: The Holy Spirit, who overshadowed the Virgin Mary, speaks to us through His written Word. In this Scripture reading He teaches us about the prophecies to the Daughter of Sion and their fulfillment in Mary. Let us be attentive as He tells us that salvation would come to the Daughter of Sion; that God Himself would come to dwell in her; and that Mary, the Daughter of Sion, would give birth to Jesus, Son of God and Saviour of the world. In preparation for our reading let us recite Proverbs 8, verses 22–31.

First Reading: The Word of God as recorded in the Book of Sophonias, chapter 3, verses 14–20. In this reading God is telling us that salvation would come to the Daughter of Sion.

¶ In grateful response to the Word we have received, let us recite Micheas 4, verses 6–10.

Second Reading: The Word of God as recorded in the Book of

Zacharias, chapter 2, verses 10–13. In this reading God is telling us that He Himself would dwell in the midst of the Daughter of Sion.

℄ In grateful response to the Word we have received, let us recite Psalm 131, verses 11–18.

Third Reading: The Word of God as recorded in the Gospel according to St. Luke, chapter 1, verses 26–38. In this reading God is telling us that Mary, who fulfilled the prophecies to the Daughter of Sion, would give birth to Jesus, the Saviour of the world.

℄ In grateful response to the Word we have received, let us recite Psalm 86, verses 1–7.

Conclusion: Let us express our deep thanks to God for Mary, the Daughter of Sion, by reciting the Hail Mary.

106. MARY AS MOTHER

Is.	7, 10–14	Sir.	24, 9–21	(Douay, 14–31)
Lk.	2, 1–7	Ct.	4, 12–16	
Jn.	19, 25–30	1 Sm. (1 Kgs.)	2, 1–10	
		Jer.	31, 10–14	

Introduction: The Holy Spirit, who overshadowed the Virgin Mary, speaks to us through His written Word. In this Scripture reading He teaches us about the Motherhood of Mary. Let us be attentive as He tells us that He promised through Isaias that the Messias would be born of a virgin; that Mary is that virgin, who became the mother of Jesus when He was born at Bethlehem; and that before Jesus died on the cross He gave Mary to us to be our Mother. In preparation for our reading let us recite Sirach 24, verses 9–21.

First Reading: The Word of God as recorded in the Book of Isaias, chapter 7, verses 10–14. In this reading God is telling us that the Messias, God-With-Us, will be born of a virgin.

℄ In grateful response to the Word we have received, let us recite Canticle of Canticles 4, verses 12–16.

Second Reading: The Word of God as recorded in the Gospel according to St. Luke, chapter 2, verses 1–7. In this reading God is telling us that the Blessed Virgin Mary became the mother of Jesus in Bethlehem.

℄ In grateful response to the Word we have received, let us recite the Canticle of Anna from the First Book of Samuel, chapter 2, verses 1–10.

Third Reading: The Word of God as recorded in the Gospel according to St. John, chapter 19, verses 25–30. In this reading God is telling us that Jesus gave us Mary to be our Mother just before He died on the cross.

℄ In grateful response to the Word we have received, let us recite the Canticle of Jeremias from the Book of Jeremias, chapter 31, verses 10–14.

Conclusion: Let us thank God sincerely for giving us Mary to be our Mother by reciting the Memorare.

107. MARY, ARK OF THE COVENANT

2 Sm. (2 Kgs.)	6, 1–9	Wis.	7, 25–8, 1
Lk.	1, 39–45	Ps.	131, 1–10
Ap.	11, 19–12, 6	Lk.	1, 46–55
		Lk.	2, 29–32

Introduction: The Holy Spirit, who overshadowed the Virgin Mary, speaks to us through His written Word. In this Scripture reading He communicates to us His teaching on Mary as the Ark of the Covenant. Let us be attentive as He tells us that the Ark of the Covenant, which was God's dwelling place in the Old Law, foreshadowed Mary, who bore the Author of the New Law; and that the Ark of the Old Law and the Ark of the New Law will be seen in their fulfillment in heaven. In preparation for our reading let us recite Wisdom 7, verse 25 to chapter 8, verse 1.

First Reading: The Word of God as recorded in the Second Book of Samuel, chapter 6, verses 1–9. In this reading God is telling us of the coming of the Ark of the Old Law to David. David asked, "How shall the Ark of the Lord come to me?"

❡ In grateful response to the Word we have received, let us recite Psalm 131, verses 1–10.

Second Reading: The Word of God as recorded in the Gospel according to St. Luke, chapter 1, verses 39–45. In this reading God is telling us of the coming of Mary, the Ark of the New Law, to Elizabeth, who asked, "How have I deserved that the Mother of my Lord should come to me?"

❡ In grateful response to the Word we have received, let us recite the Canticle of Mary from the Gospel according to St. Luke, chapter 1, verses 46–55.

Third Reading: The Word of God as recorded in the Apocalypse, chapter 11, verse 19 to chapter 12, verse 6. In this reading God is showing us the fulfillment of the Ark of the Old Law and the Ark of the New Law in heaven.

❡ In grateful response to the Word we have received, let us recite the Canticle of Simeon from the Gospel according to St. Luke, chapter 2, verses 29–32.

Conclusion: Let us express our deep thanks to God for the Virgin Mary, the Ark of the Covenant, by reciting this prayer:

Almighty, everlasting God, by the cooperation of the Holy Spirit, You prepared the body and soul of the glorious Virgin Mother, Mary, that she might become a fitting dwelling for Your Son; grant that we, who rejoice in thinking of her, may by her loving intercession be delivered from present evils and from everlasting death.

108. MARY, THE NEW EVE

Gn. 3, 1–15		Is. 51, 1–6
Jn. 2, 1–11		Pss. 129, 1–8
Jn. 19, 25–27		44, 11–18
		Lk. 1, 68–75

Introduction: The Holy Spirit, who overshadowed the Virgin Mary, speaks to us through His written Word. In this Scripture reading He communicates to us His teaching on Mary as the New Eve.

Let us be attentive as He tells us that, just as the woman, Eve, cooperated with Adam in the fall of man, so Mary, the Woman, the New Eve, cooperated with Christ, the New Adam, in the redemption of man. This redemption was announced in the Garden of Eden, was symbolized at Cana, and was perfected on Mount Calvary. In preparation for our reading let us recite Isaias 51, verses 1–6.

First Reading: The Word of God as recorded in the Book of Genesis, chapter 3, verses 1–15. In this reading God is telling us that Eve led Adam to sin, but God promised redemption through the seed of the woman.

¶ In grateful response to the Word we have received, let us recite Psalm 129, verses 1–8.

Second Reading: The Word of God as recorded in the Gospel according to St. John, chapter 2, verses 1–11. In this reading God is telling us that Mary, the Woman, the New Eve, cooperated with Christ in the miracle at Cana, a symbol of the redemption on Calvary.

¶ In grateful response to the Word we have received, let us recite Psalm 44, verses 11–18.

Third Reading: The Word of God as recorded in the Gospel according to St. John, chapter 19, verses 25–27. In this reading God is telling us that Mary, the Woman, the New Eve, cooperated with Christ on Calvary in the redemption of man.

¶ In grateful response to the Word we have received, let us recite the Canticle of Zachary from the Gospel according to St. Luke, chapter 1, verses 68–75.

Conclusion: Let us express our deep thanks to God for Mary, the New Eve, the Mother of all believers, by reciting the Hail, Holy Queen.

109. ST. PETER

Jn.	1, 35–42		Prv.	3,	13–18
Mt.	14, 22–33		Pss.	1,	1–6
Lk.	22, 54–62			17,	2–7
Acts.	12, 1–17			50,	3–14
				33,	2–11

Introduction: God, who selects men to preach His Word, instructs us through that same Word. In this Scripture reading He teaches us about St. Peter the Apostle. Let us be attentive as He tells us of the call of Peter, of his fear and failing during our Lord's ministry, and of his greatness as head of the Church after the Resurrection. In preparation for our reading let us recite Proverbs 3, verses 13–18.

First Reading: The Word of God as recorded in the Gospel according to St. John, chapter 1, verses 35–42. In this reading God is telling us that Jesus called Simon specially and changed his name to Peter.

℄ In grateful response to the Word we have received, let us recite Psalm 1, verses 1–6.

Second Reading: The Word of God as recorded in the Gospel according to St. Matthew, chapter 14, verses 22–33. In this reading God is telling us that Peter's faith was weak before the Resurrection.

℄ In response to the Word we have received, let us recite Psalm 17, verses 2–7.

Third Reading: The Word of God as recorded in the Gospel according to St. Luke, chapter 22, verses 54–62. In this reading God is telling us that Peter even denied Christ three times during His trial.

℄ In response to the Word we have received, let us recite Psalm 50, verses 3–14.

Fourth Reading: The Word of God as recorded in the Acts of the Apostles, chapter 12, verses 1–17. In this reading God is telling us that Peter, a changed man after the Resurrection, was delivered from prison while the Church prayed without ceasing for him.

℄ In grateful response to the Word we have received, let us recite Psalm 33, verses 2–11.

Conclusion: Let us thank God for instructing us on St. Peter the Apostle by reciting this prayer:

O God, You broke the bonds of the holy apostle, Peter, and led him forth in safety; by his merits break the chains of sinners, we beg You, that they may, with the whole Church, pray without ceasing.

110. THE PRIMACY OF PETER

Mt. 16, 13–19	Sir. 45, 7–13 (Douay, 8–16)
Jn. 21, 15–19	Pss. 86, 1–7
Acts 1, 15–26	22, 1–6
	23, 1–10

Introduction: God, who selects men to preach His Word, instructs us through that same Word. In this Scripture reading He communicates to us His teaching on the primacy of Peter. Let us be attentive as He tells us that Peter was promised the primacy, or first place, in the Church; that Jesus ordered Peter to this office when He commanded Peter three times to feed the flock; and that Peter acted as head of the Church as soon as Jesus ascended into heaven. In preparation for our reading let us recite Sirach 45, verses 7–13.

First Reading: The Word of God as recorded in the Gospel according to St. Matthew, chapter 16, verses 13–19. In this reading God is telling us that Jesus promised the primacy to Peter at Caesarea Philippi.

℄ In grateful response to the Word we have received, let us recite Psalm 86, verses 1–7.

Second Reading: The Word of God as recorded in the Gospel according to St. John, chapter 21, verses 15–19. In this reading God is telling us that Jesus renewed this important promise to Peter after the Resurrection. "Feed my lambs. . . . Feed my sheep."

℄ In grateful response to the Word we have received, let us recite Psalm 22, verses 1–6.

Third Reading: The Word of God as recorded in the Acts of the Apostles, chapter 1, verses 15–26. In this reading God is telling us that as soon as Jesus ascended into heaven Peter acted as head — chief shepherd — of the Church.

℄ In grateful response to the Word we have received, let us recite Psalm 23, verses 1–10.

Conclusion: Let us express our deep thanks to God for the primacy of Peter and for our present pope, Peter's successor, by reciting this prayer:

Lord Jesus Christ, You gave to Your blessed apostle, Peter, the power of binding and loosing, and the keys of the kingdom of heaven; grant that by his office as shepherd we may be led back from sin and have a full share in the mysteries of the Church.

111. ST. PETER'S PREACHING

Acts 2, 22–41	Pss. 33, 16–23
Acts 3, 12–26	15, 1–11
Acts 10, 34–43	36, 16–24
	36, 30–40

Introduction: God, who selects men to preach His Word, instructs us through that same Word. In this Scripture reading He gives us three of St. Peter's great sermons. Let us be attentive as He tells us that what is written in the Gospels was first preached by St. Peter to the early Church, namely that with Jesus Christ there came fulfillment and salvation, of which the apostles are witnesses. In preparation for our reading let us recite Psalm 33, verses 16–23.

First Reading: The Word of God as recorded in the Acts of the Apostles, chapter 2, verses 22–41. In this reading God is telling us through Peter's preaching that Christ, fulfilling David's prophecy, rose from the dead, and shares His new life with us.

℄ In grateful response to the Word we have received, let us recite Psalm 15, verses 1–11.

Second Reading: The Word of God as recorded in the Acts of the Apostles, chapter 3, verses 12–26. In this reading God is telling us through St. Peter's preaching to repent and believe in the Passion, death, and Resurrection of Jesus Christ in order to be saved.

In grateful response to the Word we have received, let us recite Psalm 36, verses 16–24.

Third Reading: The Word of God as recorded in the Acts of the Apostles, chapter 10, verses 34–43. In this reading God is telling us that the apostles are witnesses to the power of the Lord Jesus as the Appointed One of God.

In grateful response to the Word we have received, let us recite Psalm 36, verses 30–40.

Conclusion: Let us express our deep thanks to God for the preaching of St. Peter by reciting the following prayer:

O God, You bestowed upon blessed Peter the power to preach the Good News of salvation; grant that by his intercession we may have a fuller share in the Passion, death, and Resurrection of Jesus Christ, Your Son.

112. ST. PAUL

Jer.	1,	4–10	Jb.	5,	17–27
Acts	9,	1–19	Jer.	31,	10–14
2 Cor.	11,	21–33	Pss.	3,	2–9
2 Tm.	4,	1–8		142,	1–12
				116,	1–2

Introduction: God, who selects men to preach His Word, instructs us through that same Word. In this Scripture reading He teaches us about St. Paul. Let us be attentive as He tells us about the call, the conversion, the sufferings, and the "good fight" of St. Paul, Apostle to the Gentiles. In preparation for our reading let us recite Job 5, verses 17–27.

First Reading: The Word of God as recorded in the Book of Jeremias, chapter 1, verses 4–10. In this reading God is telling us about Jeremias' call, which reminds us so beautifully of the mission of St. Paul.

In grateful response to the Word we have received, let us recite the Canticle of Jeremias from the Book of Jeremias, chapter 31, verses 10–14.

Second Reading: The Word of God as recorded in the Acts of the Apostles, chapter 9, verses 1–19. In this reading God is telling us of the sudden conversion of St. Paul and his mission to the Gentiles.

℄ In grateful response to the Word we have received, let us recite Psalm 3, verses 2–9.

Third Reading: The Word of God as recorded in the Second Epistle to the Corinthians, chapter 11, verses 21–33. In this reading God is telling us how much St. Paul had to suffer to accomplish his mission to the Gentiles.

℄ In grateful response to the Word we have received, let us recite Psalm 142, verses 1–12.

Fourth Reading: The Word of God as recorded in the Second Epistle to Timothy, chapter 4, verses 1–8. In this reading God is telling us that St. Paul at the end of his life, after having "fought the good fight," urged Timothy, his disciple, to preach the Word of God.

℄ In grateful response to the Word we have received, let us recite Psalm 116, verses 1–2.

Conclusion: Let us thank God for giving to His Church St. Paul, the greatest missionary of all times, by reciting this prayer:

O God, You taught the whole world by the preaching of St. Paul, the Apostle; grant that we, who continue to celebrate his efforts for the Church, may by following his example come closer to You.

113. ST. JOHN, SON OF ZEBEDEE

Mt. 4, 18–22	Wis. 6, 22–7, 14 (Douay, 6, 24–7, 14)
Jn. 19, 25–30	Pss. 61, 2–9
Jn. 21, 20–25	65, 1–12
	64, 2–5

Introduction: God, who selects men to preach His Word, instructs us through that same Word. In this Scripture reading He communicates to us His teaching on St. John. Let us be attentive as He tells us that St. John was among the first disciples called by Christ, that St. John was the faithful disciple to whom Jesus entrusted His Blessed

Mother, and that St. John is the beloved witness of Jesus. In preparation for our reading let us recite Wisdom 6, verse 22 to chapter 7, verse 14.

First Reading: The Word of God as recorded in the Gospel according to St. Matthew, chapter 4, verses 18–22. In this reading God is telling us that St. John was among the first four disciples called by Jesus.

℄ In grateful response to the Word we have received, let us recite Psalm 61, verses 2–9.

Second Reading: The Word of God as recorded in the Gospel according to St. John, chapter 19, verses 25–30. In this reading God is telling us that Jesus entrusted His Blessed Mother to His beloved disciple, St. John.

℄ In grateful response to the Word we have received, let us recite Psalm 65, verses 1–12.

Third Reading: The Word of God as recorded in the Gospel according to St. John, chapter 21, verses 20–25. In this reading God is telling us that St. John is the beloved witness of Jesus.

℄ In grateful response to the Word we have received, let us recite Psalm 64, verses 2–5.

Conclusion: Let us express our deep thanks to God for St. John, the Beloved Disciple, by reciting this prayer:

Graciously enlighten Your Church, O Lord, that being instructed by the teaching of St. John, Your apostle and evangelist, she may win everlasting gifts.

114. MARTYRS

2 Mc.	7, 1–6	Wis.	3, 1–9
Mt.	10, 26–39	Pss.	137, 1–8
Acts	7, 54–60		118, 1–8
			23, 1–10

Introduction: God, who selects men to preach His Word, instructs us through that same Word. In this Scripture reading He communicates to us His teaching on martyrs. Let us be attentive as He tells us that martyrdom is beautifully portrayed in the Old Testament by a whole family which died for its faith; that Jesus taught that men must be willing to lose their life for His sake; and that a magnificent example of heroic self-sacrifice is the first martyr, St. Stephen. In preparation for our reading let us recite Wisdom 3, verses 1–9.

First Reading: The Word of God as recorded in the Second Book of Machabees, chapter 7, verses 1–6. In this reading God is telling us that for the love of Him a Jewish mother and her seven sons gave up their lives during a terrible persecution.

℄ In grateful response to the Word we have received, let us recite Psalm 137, verses 1–8.

Second Reading: The Word of God as recorded in the Gospel according to St. Matthew, chapter 10, verses 26–39. In this reading God is telling us that, according to Jesus' teaching, one should sacrifice his life, if necessary, for the love of Him.

℄ In grateful response to the Word we have received, let us recite Psalm 118, verses 1–8.

Third Reading: The Word of God as recorded in the Acts of the Apostles, chapter 7, verses 54–60. In this reading God is telling us that St. Stephen laid down his life out of love for God.

℄ In grateful response to the Word we have received, let us recite Psalm 23, verses 1–10.

Conclusion: Let us express our deep thanks to God for His martyrs, who have been heroic witnesses to Him in their blood, by reciting this prayer:

O God, You give us the opportunity in the church year to celebrate the heavenly birthdays of Your holy martyrs; grant us, we pray, the grace to enjoy some day their companionship in heaven.

115. CONFESSORS

Sir.	39, 1–11 (Douay, 1–15)	Pss.	1,	1–6
Lk.	12, 35–40		91,	13–16
Mt.	25, 14–23		111,	1–10
		Prv.	3,	13–18

Introduction: God our Father speaks to us through His living Word. In this Scripture reading He teaches us about confessors, that is, about those who confess that Jesus is Lord and persevere in that confession. Let us be attentive as He tells us a confessor is one who has treasured Him more than the riches of the world, who lives the command of Jesus to be ever watchful, and who will enjoy a great reward on Judgment Day. In preparation for our reading let us recite Psalm 1, verses 1–6.

First Reading: The Word of God as recorded in the Book of Sirach, chapter 39, verses 1–11. In this reading God is telling us that the confessor puts his trust in God and not in riches.

¶ In grateful response to the Word we have received, let us recite Psalm 91, verses 13–16.

Second Reading: The Word of God as recorded in the Gospel according to St. Luke, chapter 12, verses 35–40. In this reading God is telling us that the confessor is one who is ever waiting for the Lord to come.

¶ In grateful response to the Word we have received, let us recite Psalm 111, verses 1–10.

Third Reading: The Word of God as recorded in the Gospel according to St. Matthew, chapter 25, verses 14–23. In this reading God is telling us that the confessor will receive a great reward for doing the will of his Master.

¶ In grateful response to the Word we have received, let us recite Proverbs 3, verses 13–18.

Conclusion: Let us express our deep thanks to God for His saintly confessors by reciting the Our Father.

116. VIRGINS

1 Cor.	7,	25–35	Pss.	90,	1–13
Mt.	25,	1–13		118,	9–16
Lk.	1,	26–38		62,	2–9
			Lk.	1,	46–55

Introduction: The Holy Spirit, who overshadowed the Virgin Mary, speaks to us through His written Word. In this Scripture reading He communicates to us His teaching on virgins. Let us be attentive as He tells us about the nature and beauty of consecrated virginity, the necessity for virgins to be watchful, and the ideal of this perfect virginity which is found in the Blessed Virgin. In preparation for our reading let us recite Psalm 90, verses 1–13.

First Reading: The Word of God as recorded in the First Epistle to the Corinthians, chapter 7, verses 25–35. In this reading God is telling us about the nature and beauty of consecrated virginity.

¶ In grateful response to the Word we have received, let us recite Psalm 118, verses 9–16.

Second Reading: The Word of God as recorded in the Gospel according to St. Matthew, chapter 25, verses 1–13. In this reading God is telling us that virgins must ever watch for the coming of Christ.

¶ In grateful response to the Word we have received, let us recite Psalm 62, verses 2–9.

Third Reading: The Word of God as recorded in the Gospel according to St. Luke, chapter 1, verses 26–38. In this reading God is telling us that the Blessed Virgin is the ideal of perfect, consecrated virginity.

¶ In grateful response to the Word we have received, let us recite the Canticle of Mary from the Gospel according to St. Luke, chapter 1, verses 46–55.

Conclusion: Let us express our deep thanks to God for His teaching on virginity by reciting the Hail Mary.

117. HOLY WOMEN IN THE BIBLE

Jdt.	8, 1–17	Ps.	8, 2–10	
Est.	14, 1–19	Jdt.	16, 13–17	(Douay, 15–21)
Jn.	20, 1–18	1 Sm. (1 Kgs.)	2, 1–10	
		Ps.	44, 11–18	

Introduction: God our Father speaks to us through His living Word. In this Scripture reading He instructs us on holy women in the Bible. Let us be attentive as He tells us of Judith, Esther, and Mary Magdalene. In preparation for our reading let us recite Psalm 8, verses 2–10.

First Reading: The Word of God as recorded in the Book of Judith, chapter 8, verses 1–17. In this reading God is telling us that Judith, a holy woman, pleaded with her countrymen to trust in God, who will deliver His people.

⁋ In grateful response to the Word we have received, let us recite the Canticle of Judith from the Book of Judith, chapter 16, verses 13–17.

Second Reading: The Word of God as recorded in the Book of Esther, chapter 14, verses 1–19. In this reading God is telling us that Esther, a holy queen, prayed for her people that they might escape persecution and slavery.

⁋ In grateful response to the Word we have received, let us recite the Canticle of Anna from the First Book of Samuel, chapter 2, verses 1–10.

Third Reading: The Word of God as recorded in the Gospel according to St. John, chapter 20, verses 1–18. In this reading God is telling us that Jesus appeared on the day of His Resurrection to Mary Magdalene, the holy woman who loved Him so much.

⁋ In grateful response to the Word we have received, let us recite Psalm 44, verses 11–18.

Conclusion: Let us thank God for His instruction on holy women in the Bible by reciting this prayer:

Graciously hear us, God, our Saviour, that as we rejoice in the good works of these holy women we may learn to love You all the more.

118. THE FOLLOWING OF CHRIST

Mt. 5, 1–12		Pss. 130, 1–3	
Mk. 10, 46–52		77, 1–7	
Lk. 10, 25–37		39, 2–6	
		31, 8–11	

Introduction: In Sacred Scripture God is ever telling us of His Divine Word. In this Scripture reading He communicates to us His teaching on the following of Christ. Let us be attentive as He tells us that Jesus set up an ideal which all His true followers should try to observe; furthermore, He tells us that we must have great faith in Christ, like Bartimeus, if we want to follow Him; and finally the true follower of Christ, like the Good Samaritan, must strive especially to practice love of neighbor. In preparation for our reading let us recite Psalm 130, verses 1–3.

First Reading: The Word of God as recorded in the Gospel according to St. Matthew, chapter 5, verses 1–12. In this reading God is telling us how Jesus in a beautiful sermon described His ideal follower.

℄ In grateful response to the Word we have received, let us recite Psalm 77, verses 1–7.

Second Reading: The Word of God as recorded in the Gospel according to St. Mark, chapter 10, verses 46–52. In this reading God is telling us that we must have faith like Bartimeus, if we are to follow Christ.

℄ In grateful response to the Word we have received, let us recite Psalm 39, verses 2–6.

Third Reading: The Word of God as recorded in the Gospel according to St. Luke, chapter 10, verses 25–37. In this reading God is telling us that to be followers of Christ we must strive especially to practice love of neighbor.

℄ In grateful response to the Word we have received, let us recite Psalm 31, verses 8–11.

Conclusion: Let us thank God for His words on the following of Christ by reciting this prayer:

O Lord, You have promised a hundredfold reward and life everlasting to those who leave all and follow You; give us the strength to despise earthly wealth and to store up treasures only in heaven.

119. HEARING THE WORD OF GOD

Lk. 8, 4–15	Is. 55, 6–11
Mt. 7, 21–29	Ps. 118, 9–16
Jas. 1, 19–25	118, 17–24
	118, 25–32

Introduction: The Holy Spirit, who has entrusted His living Word to the Church, speaks to us. In this Scripture reading He teaches us about hearing the Word of God and acting on it. Let us be attentive as He tells us that we must have the proper disposition to receive the Word of God faithfully, and that we should make the Word of God influence our daily lives as "doers of the Word, and not hearers only." In preparation for our reading let us recite Isaias 55, verses 6–11.

First Reading: The Word of God as recorded in the Gospel according to St. Luke, chapter 8, verses 4–15. In this reading God is telling us through the Parable of the Sower that, to hear His word fruitfully, we must dispose ourselves with "a right and good heart."
℄ In grateful response to the Word we have received, let us recite Psalm 118, verses 9–16.

Second Reading: The Word of God as recorded in the Gospel according to St. Matthew, chapter 7, verses 21–29. In this reading God is telling us that hearing His Word is not enough for salvation. We must make that Word influence our daily actions.
℄ In grateful response to the Word we have received, let us recite Psalm 118, verses 17–24.

Third Reading: The Word of God as recorded in the Epistle of St. James, chapter 1, verses 19–25. In this reading God is telling us through St. James that we who have received the Word of God should try to be "doers of the Word, and not hearers only"—we should try to understand it better and obey it.

◖ In grateful response to the Word we have received, let us recite Psalm 118, verses 25–32.

Conclusion: Let us express our deep thanks to God for teaching us His Word, and with this prayer let us ask Him to make us "doers of the Word":

O God, Your Divine Son has pronounced "blessed" those who hear the Word of God and keep it; grant that we, Your People, may always listen to Your Word with attention, and, being guided by the light of the Holy Spirit, learn to act upon it.

120. PRAYER

Ex.	17, 8–14	Pss.	4, 2–9
Lk.	11, 1–13		107, 2–7
Lk.	18, 1–14		114, 1–9
			122, 1–4

Introduction: God our Father instructs us through His living Word. In this Scripture reading He teaches us about prayer. Let us be attentive as He tells us of the power of prayer and of the necessity of praying with perseverance and humility. In preparation for our reading let us recite Psalm 4, verses 2–9.

First Reading: The Word of God as recorded in the Book of Exodus, chapter 17, verses 8–14. In this reading God is telling us that, as long as Moses would pray, the Israelites were successful in battle.

◖ In grateful response to the Word we have received, let us recite Psalm 107, verses 2–7.

Second Reading: The Word of God as recorded in the Gospel according to St. Luke, chapter 11, verses 1–13. In this reading God is telling us through His Son how to pray and the necessity of praying with perseverance.

◖ In grateful response to the Word we have received, let us recite Psalm 114, verses 1–9.

Third Reading: The Word of God as recorded in the Gospel ac-

cording to St. Luke, chapter 18, verses 1–14. In this reading God is telling us that the publican's prayer was heard because it was the prayer of a humble heart.

℄ In grateful response to the Word we have received, let us recite Psalm 122, verses 1–4.

Conclusion: Let us thank God for His instruction on prayer by reciting together the Our Father.

121. PRAYER IN COMMON

Mt.	18, 19–20	Pss.	121, 1–9
Mk.	14, 32–42		132, 1–3
Acts	2, 37–47		129, 1–8
			135, 1–26

Introduction: God our Father speaks to us through His living Word. In this Scripture reading He instructs us on the value of prayer in common. Let us be attentive as He tells us that Jesus taught His disciples the value of praying together; He urged them to pray together with Him during His agony in the garden. We see how the early Church worshiped together "in the communion of the breaking of bread and in prayers." In preparation for our reading let us recite Psalm 121, verses 1–9.

First Reading: The Word of God as recorded in the Gospel according to St. Matthew, chapter 18, verses 19–20. In this reading God is telling us through His Son the value and power of united prayer.

℄ In grateful response to the Word we have received, let us recite Psalm 132, verses 1–3.

Second Reading: The Word of God as recorded in the Gospel according to St. Mark, chapter 14, verses 32–42. In this reading God is telling us that His Son, during His agony in the garden, urged His disciples to watch and pray together with Him.

℄ In grateful response to the Word we have received, let us recite Psalm 129, verses 1–8.

Third Reading: The Word of God as recorded in the Acts of the Apostles, chapter 2, verses 37–47. In this reading God is telling us that, after the three thousand became Christians on Pentecost, they worshiped and prayed in common.

℄ In grateful response to the Word we have received, let us recite Psalm 135, verses 1–26.

Conclusion: Let us express our deep thanks to God for His instruction on the value of praying in common by reciting together the prayer His Son has given us: the Our Father.

122. FASTING

Jon.	3,	1–10	Jl.	2,	12–17
Mt.	4,	1–11	Pss.	50,	3–14
Mt.	6,	16–18		90,	1–16
				68,	6–14

Introduction: God, who rewards the just and punishes the evil, speaks to us through His living Word. In this Scripture reading He teaches us about fasting. Let us be attentive as He tells us that fasting moves God to have mercy on our sins; that Jesus gave an example of the importance of fasting; and that our fasting should be only before God and not for men to see. In preparation for our reading let us recite Joel 2, verses 12–17.

First Reading: The Word of God as recorded in the Book of Jonas, chapter 3, verses 1–10. In this reading God is telling us, through the example of the Ninevites, that fasting moves God to have mercy on sinners.

℄ In grateful response to the Word we have received, let us recite Psalm 50, verses 3–14.

Second Reading: The Word of God as recorded in the Gospel according to St. Matthew, chapter 4, verses 1–11. In this reading God is telling us that Jesus fasted for forty days as an example to us.

℄ In grateful response to the Word we have received, let us recite Psalm 90, verses 1–16.

Third Reading: The Word of God as recorded in the Gospel according to St. Matthew, chapter 6, verses 16–18. In this reading God is telling us that our fasting should not be performed before men but only in secret before the Father in heaven.

❨ In grateful response to the Word we have received, let us recite Psalm 68, verses 6–14.

Conclusion: Let us thank God for teaching us the value of fasting by reciting this prayer:

Almighty and everlasting God, You pardoned the people of Nineveh when they fasted and put on sackcloth and ashes; help us, we pray, to turn from our evil ways and to obtain Your forgiveness.

123. GOOD EXAMPLE

2 Mc.	6, 18–31	Pss.	1, 1–6
Jn.	13, 1–15		63, 2–11
1 Pt.	2, 11–25		25, 1–12
			111, 1–10

Introduction: God our Father instructs us through His living Word. In this Scripture reading He gives us His teaching on good example. Let us be attentive as He shows us that Eleazar died giving good example; that Christ gave the apostles His example; and that St. Peter emphasizes the importance of good example. In preparation for our reading let us recite Psalm 1, verses 1–6.

First Reading: The Word of God as recorded in the Second Book of Machabees, chapter 6, verses 18–31. In this reading God is telling us that Eleazar died giving good example.

❨ In grateful response to the Word we have received, let us recite Psalm 63, verses 2–11.

Second Reading: The Word of God as recorded in the Gospel according to St. John, chapter 13, verses 1–15. In this reading God is telling us that Christ gave His apostles His example of love.

❨ In grateful response to the Word we have received, let us recite Psalm 25, verses 1–12.

Third Reading: The Word of God as recorded in the First Epistle of St. Peter, chapter 2, verses 11–25. In this reading God is telling us that St. Peter emphasized the importance of good works as an example to others in imitation of Christ.

℄ In grateful response to the Word we have received, let us recite Psalm 111, verses 1–10.

Conclusion: Let us express our thanks to God for His teaching on good example by reciting this prayer:

O God, You sent Your Son to redeem us and to leave an example that we may follow in His steps; grant that we may let our light shine before men, so that they may glorify God on the day of visitation.

124. WORK

Gn.	3,	1–19	Pss.	127,	1–6
Lk.	19,	11–27		129,	1–8
2 Thes.	3,	6–12		61,	10–13
				89,	12–17

Introduction: God, who rewards the just and punishes the evil, speaks to us through His living Word. In this Scripture reading He teaches us about work. Let us be attentive as He tells us of the place of work in man's life: for his sin man must work in the sweat of his brow; he must work out his salvation by using all his gifts of mind and body; if he does not work and share the burden, neither let him eat. In preparation for our reading let us recite Psalm 127, verses 1–6.

First Reading: The Word of God as recorded in the Book of Genesis, chapter 3, verses 1–19. In this reading God is telling us that for his sin man must work in the sweat of his brow.

℄ In response to the Word we have received, let us recite Psalm 129, verses 1–8.

Second Reading: The Word of God as recorded in the Gospel according to St. Luke, chapter 19, verses 11–27. In this reading God is telling us that each must work out his salvation with the intellectual and physical gifts God gives him.

◖ In grateful response to the Word we have received, let us recite Psalm 61, verses 10–13.

Third Reading: The Word of God as recorded in the Second Epistle to the Thessalonians, chapter 3, verses 6–12. In this reading God is telling us that St. Paul insisted that every one must work and share the burden, as he did. "If any man will not work, neither let him eat."

◖ In response to the Word we have received, let us recite Psalm 89, verses 12–17.

Conclusion: Let us thank God for this instruction on work, and let us ask Him to give us conviction on the value of work with this prayer:

O God, You ordered man because of his sin to earn his living by the sweat of his brow; give us, we pray, the light to see the value of work in Your divine plan, so we may by our perseverance work out our salvation.

125. FAITH

Gn.	15,	1–6	Ps.	3,	2–9	
Rom.	4,	18–25	Sir.	44,	19–21	(Douay, 20–23)
1 Jn.	5,	1–5	Ps.	61,	2–9	
			Lk.	2,	29–32	

Introduction: God our Father instructs us through His living Word. In this Scripture reading He communicates to us His teaching on faith. Let us be attentive as He tells us that Abraham is our model of faith; that we, the spiritual sons of Abraham, must believe in God; and that this is the victory that overcomes the world: our faith. In preparation for our reading let us recite Psalm 3, verses 2–9.

First Reading: The Word of God as recorded in the Book of Genesis, chapter 15, verses 1–6. In this reading God is telling us of Abraham's great faith in God — so great that he has become the spiritual father of all believers.

◖ In grateful response to the Word we have received, let us recite Sirach 44, verses 19–21.

Second Reading: The Word of God as recorded in the Epistle to the Romans, chapter 4, verses 18–25. In this reading God is telling us, the spiritual sons of Abraham, that we must believe in God, and in His wonderful redemption of man through Christ.

℄ In grateful response to the Word we have received, let us recite Psalm 61, verses 2–9.

Third Reading: The Word of God as recorded in the First Epistle of St. John, chapter 5, verses 1–5. In this reading God is telling us that faith will lead to a love of God, which will help us conquer the evil in the world around us and draw us to heaven.

℄ In grateful response to the Word we have received, let us recite the Canticle of Simeon from the Gospel according to St. Luke, chapter 2, verses 29–32.

Conclusion: Let us thank God for the gift of faith and recite the Apostles' Creed.

126. HOPE

Wis. 3,	1–9	Sir.	2,	6–11 (Douay, 6–13)
Mt. 6,	25–34	Pss.	30,	2–9
Ti. 2,	11–15		103,	10–18
		Mi.	7,	7–9

Introduction: God our Father instructs us through His living Word. In this Scripture reading He communicates to us His teaching on the virtue of hope. Let us be attentive as He tells us to hope in Him alone, for the souls of the just are in the hands of Him, who ever provides for us, and whose Son, Jesus Christ, is our hope in His Second Coming. In preparation for our reading let us recite Sirach 2, verses 6–11.

First Reading: The Word of God as recorded in the Book of Wisdom, chapter 3, verses 1–9. In this reading God is telling us that the just have hope, for their souls are in the hands of God.

℄ In grateful response to the Word we have received, let us recite Psalm 30, verses 2–9.

Second Reading: The Word of God as recorded in the Gospel according to St. Matthew, chapter 6, verses 25–34. In this reading God is telling us through His Son to fix our hope in Him alone.

℄ In grateful response to the Word we have received, let us recite Psalm 103, verses 10–18.

Third Reading: The Word of God as recorded in the Epistle to Titus, chapter 2, verses 11–15. In this reading God is telling us that we should live good lives as we await with hope the glorious Second Coming of Jesus Christ.

℄ In grateful response to the Word we have received, let us recite Micheas 7, verses 7–9.

Conclusion: Let us express our thanks to God for giving us hope in Jesus Christ, His Son, by reciting the following prayer:

O God, the strength of those who trust in You, provide generously for Your people in this life, that at Your Son's Second Coming we may be numbered among the elect.

127. CHARITY: THE LOVE OF GOD

Dt.	6,	1–9		Pss.	114,	1–9
Mk.	12,	28–34			18,	8–11
1 Jn.	4,	7–11			30,	20–25
				Sir.	34,	13–17 (Douay, 14–20)

Introduction: God our Father speaks to us through His living Word. In this Scripture reading He communicates to us His teaching on charity, the love of God. Let us be attentive as He tells us that we must love God above all else because He has first loved us. In preparation for our reading let us recite Psalm 114, verses 1–9.

First Reading: The Word of God as recorded in the Book of Deuteronomy, chapter 6, verses 1–9. In this reading God is exhorting us to love Him with all our heart, and with all our soul, and with all our strength.

℄ In grateful response to the Word we have received, let us recite Psalm 18, verses 8–11.

Second Reading: The Word of God as recorded in the Gospel according to St. Mark, chapter 12, verses 28–34. In this reading God is telling us that love of God and neighbor is the great commandment.

⸿ In grateful response to the Word we have received, let us recite Psalm 30, verses 20–25.

Third Reading: The Word of God as recorded in the First Epistle of St. John, chapter 4, verses 7–11. In this reading God is telling us that we must love God and neighbor because He has first loved us.

⸿ In grateful response to the Word we have received, let us recite Sirach 34, verses 13–17.

Conclusion: Let us express our deep thanks to God for His teaching on charity by reciting this prayer:
Where charity and love are, there God is;
The love of Christ brings us together as one.
Let us exult and rejoice in Him;
Let us fear and love the living God;
Let us love one another from the depths of our hearts.

128. CHARITY: THE LOVE OF NEIGHBOR

Lv.	19,	13–18
Mt.	5,	43–48
1 Cor.	13,	1–13

Pss.	14,	1–5
	111,	1–9
Sir.	3,	29–4, 10 (Douay, 3, 33–4, 11)
Ps.	132,	1–3

Introduction: God our Father instructs us through His living Word. In this Scripture reading He gives us His teaching on love of neighbor. Let us be attentive as He tells us how important it is to have love in our hearts — love not only for our friends but even for our enemies. In preparation for our reading let us recite Psalm 14, verses 1–5.

First Reading: The Word of God as recorded in the Book of Leviticus, chapter 19, verses 13–18. In this reading God is telling us that we must not hate our neighbor but love him as ourselves.

⸿ In grateful response to the Word we have received, let us recite Psalm 111, verses 1–9.

Second Reading: The Word of God as recorded in the Gospel according to St. Matthew, chapter 5, verses 43–48. In this reading God is telling us that we are obliged to love not only our friends but even to love those who persecute us.

℄ In grateful response to the Word we have received, let us recite Sirach 3, verse 29 to chapter 4, verse 10.

Third Reading: The Word of God as recorded in the First Epistle to the Corinthians, chapter 13, verses 1–13. In this reading God is telling us of the excellence of charity; love of God and neighbor is the greatest virtue of all.

℄ In grateful response to the Word we have received, let us recite Psalm 132, verses 1–3.

Conclusion: Let us express our deep thanks to God for His teaching on charity by reciting the following prayer:

Where charity and love are, there God is.
Therefore when we are together, let us take heed not to be divided in mind.
Let there be an end to bitterness and quarrels,
And let Christ our God dwell in the midst of us.

129. HUMILITY

Sir.	3,	17–28 (Douay, 19–32)	Pss.	33,	2–11
Lk.	14,	7–11		130,	1–3
Lk.	18,	9–14		146,	1–6
Phil.	2,	1–11		112,	1–9
				102,	13–18

Introduction: God, who rewards the just and punishes the evil, speaks to us through His living Word. In this Scripture reading He communicates to us His teaching on the virtue of humility. Let us be attentive as He tells us that by humility we will find favor with God; and that he who humbles himself will be exalted, just as Christ, who humbled Himself on the cross, was gloriously exalted in His Resurrection. In preparation for our reading, let us recite Psalm 33, verses 2–11.

First Reading: The Word of God as recorded in the Book of Sirach, chapter 3, verses 17–28. In this reading God is telling us that by humbly recognizing our limitations we will make ourselves pleasing to Him.

℄ In grateful response to the Word we have received, let us recite Psalm 130, verses 1–3.

Second Reading: The Word of God as recorded in the Gospel according to St. Luke, chapter 14, verses 7–11. In this reading God is telling us that humility prefers the lowest place.

℄ In grateful response to the Word we have received, let us recite Psalm 146, verses 1–6.

Third Reading: The Word of God as recorded in the Gospel according to St. Luke, chapter 18, verses 9–14. In this reading God is telling us that humility means recognizing ourselves as sinners in His sight.

℄ In grateful response to the Word we have received, let us recite Psalm 112, verses 1–9.

Fourth Reading: The Word of God as recorded in the Epistle to the Philippians, chapter 2, verses 1–11. In this reading God is telling us that we should imitate Christ Jesus, who humbled Himself even to death on the cross and was gloriously exalted in His Resurrection.

℄ In grateful response to the Word we have received, let us recite Psalm 102, verses 13–18.

Conclusion: Let us ask God to teach us to be humble by reciting this prayer:

O God, Your Son has taught us by word to be meek and humble of heart, and by example to humble ourselves as He did even to death on the cross; give us, we pray, the grace and strength to unite ourselves to Him in His Passion so as to be sharers in His Resurrection.

130. POVERTY

Lk. 2, 1–7	Jb. 24, 2–12
Lk. 6, 17–26	Lk. 1, 46–55
Lk. 14, 15–24	Ps. 36, 10–22
	So. 3, 11–13

Introduction: God our Father instructs us through His living Word. In this Scripture reading He teaches us about poverty. Let us be attentive as He tells us that His Son, Jesus Christ, was born in poverty, declared the poor to be "blessed," and to be the members of His messianic kingdom. In preparation for our reading let us recite Job 24, verses 2–12.

First Reading: The Word of God as recorded in the Gospel according to St. Luke, chapter 2, verses 1–7. In this reading God is telling us that Jesus Christ was born in poverty, wrapped in swaddling clothes, and laid in a manger.

℄ In grateful response to the Word we have received, let us recite the Canticle of Mary from the Gospel according to St. Luke, chapter 1, verses 46–55.

Second Reading: The Word of God as recorded in the Gospel according to St. Luke, chapter 6, verses 17–26. In this reading God is telling us that the poor are "blessed," for they are members of His messianic kingdom.

℄ In grateful response to the Word we have received, let us recite Psalm 36, verses 10–22.

Third Reading: The Word of God as recorded in the Gospel according to St. Luke, chapter 14, verses 15–24. In this reading God is telling us that at the messianic banquet it is the poor, the crippled, the blind, and the lame who will be invited.

℄ In grateful response to the Word we have received, let us recite Sophonias 3, verses 11–13.

Conclusion: Let us give thanks to God for His teaching on poverty with this prayer:

O Lord Jesus Christ, You, the Saviour of the world, became poor as an example to us; graciously give us, we pray, the spirit of detachment from worldly goods, so that we may share in Your messianic feast in heaven.

131. THE FIRST COMMANDMENT

Jer. 10, 1–16	Is. 45, 15–25	
Dn. 14, 22–42	Sir. 1, 9–18	(Douay, 11–25)
Acts 17, 22–31	Ps. 134, 15–21	
	Ps. 96, 1–12	

Introduction: God our Father instructs us through His living Word. In this Scripture reading He teaches us the First Commandment: "I, the Lord, am your God. You shall not have other gods besides me." Let us be attentive at He tells us of the folly of idolatry and the wisdom of worshiping the one, true God. In preparation for our reading let us recite the Canticle of Isaias from the Book of Isaias, chapter 45, verses 15–25.

First Reading: The Word of God as recorded in the Book of Jeremias, chapter 10, verses 1–16. In this reading God is telling us that the worship of idols is stupid and senseless, but the worship of the Lord God is true religion.

℄ In grateful response to the Word we have received, let us recite Sirach 1, verses 9–18.

Second Reading: The Word of God as recorded in the Book of Daniel, chapter 14, verses 22–42. In this reading God is telling us that Daniel refused to worship the dragon-god and was rewarded for his fidelity by deliverance from the lions' den.

℄ In grateful response to the Word we have received, let us recite Psalm 134, verses 15–21.

Third Reading: The Word of God as recorded in the Acts of the Apostles, chapter 17, verses 22–31. In this reading God is telling us that St. Paul at Athens preached the true worship of the one God and the folly of idol-worship.

℄ In grateful response to the Word we have received, let us recite Psalm 96, verses 1–12.

Conclusion: Let us express our deep thanks to the one, true God for giving us the grace to worship Him alone, and let us make the act of adoration by reciting this prayer from the Canon of the Mass:

Through Him, and with Him, and in Him
You receive, God the Father almighty,
In the unity of the Holy Spirit,
All honor and glory, through all ages.
Amen.

132. THE SECOND COMMANDMENT

Sir. 23, 7–15 (Douay, 7–20)
Mt. 5, 33–37
Mt. 26, 69–75

Pss. 23, 1–6
51, 3–7
14, 1–5
50, 3–11

Introduction: God, who rewards the good and punishes the evil, speaks to us through His living Word. In this Scripture reading He instructs us on the Second Commandment: "You shall not take the name of the Lord, your God, in vain." Let us be attentive as He tells us that we must revere His holy name and not swear falsely by it as did St. Peter in his denial of Christ. In preparation for our reading let us recite Psalm 23, verses 1–6.

First Reading: The Word of God as recorded in the Book of Sirach, chapter 23, verses 7–15. In this reading God is telling us that the man who swears in vain commits a sin and will not go unpunished.

℄ In response to the Word we have received, let us recite Psalm 51, verses 3–7.

Second Reading: The Word of God as recorded in the Gospel according to St. Matthew, chapter 5, verses 33–37. In this reading God is telling us that Christ, His Son, stressed the importance of not swearing by God's holy name nor by the things which belong to God.

℄ In grateful response to the Word we have received, let us recite Psalm 14, verses 1–5.

Third Reading: The Word of God as recorded in the Gospel ac-

cording to St. Matthew, chapter 26, verses 69–75. In this reading God is telling us that St. Peter swore by an oath that he did not know Jesus and committed a grievous sin for which he wept bitterly.

¶ In response to the Word we have received, let us recite Psalm 50, verses 3–11.

Conclusion: Let us thank God for teaching us the Second Commandment, and let us think specially on the words "hallowed be Thy name," as we recite the Our Father.

133. THE THIRD COMMANDMENT

Gn.	1,	26–2, 3	Is.	56,	1–8
Dt.	5,	12–15	Ps.	145,	1–10
Mk.	2,	23–28	Jer.	17,	24–27
Mt.	28,	1–10	Pss.	99,	1–5
				121,	1–9

Introduction: God our Father speaks to us through His living Word. In this Scripture reading He instructs us on the Third Commandment: "Keep holy the Sabbath Day." Let us be attentive as He tells us that after six days of creation He blessed the seventh day by resting; that the Sabbath was the day which Israel dedicated to God in thanksgiving for deliverance from Egypt; and that His Son, Jesus Christ, is the Lord of the Sabbath, especially by His Resurrection on the first day of the week. In preparation for our reading let us recite Isaias 56, verses 1–8.

First Reading: The Word of God as recorded in the Book of Genesis, chapter 1, verse 26 to chapter 2, verse 3. In this reading God is telling us that after six days of creation He blessed the seventh day by resting from His work.

¶ In grateful response to the Word we have received, let us recite Psalm 145, verses 1–10.

Second Reading: The Word of God as recorded in the Book of Deuteronomy, chapter 5, verses 12–15. In this reading God is telling us that the Sabbath was the day above all on which the Israelites were to rest and recall the redemption from Egypt.

¶ In grateful response to the Word we have received, let us recite Jeremias 17, verses 24–27.

Third Reading: The Word of God as recorded in the Gospel according to St. Mark, chapter 2, verses 23–28. In this reading God is telling us that Jesus Christ, His Son, is Lord even of the Sabbath.

¶ In grateful response to the Word we have received, let us recite Psalm 99, verses 1–5.

Fourth Reading: The Word of God as recorded in the Gospel according to St. Matthew, chapter 28, verses 1–10. In this reading God is telling us that our Sabbath, the first day of the week, was made holy once and for all time by the Resurrection of Christ.

¶ In grateful response to the Word we have received, let us recite Psalm 121, verses 1–9.

Conclusion: Let us express our deep thanks to God for showing us the sacredness of the Lord's Day by reciting this prayer:

O God, who wondrously re-created the universe by the blessed Resurrection of Your Son on the first day of the week, grant that we, Your people, may obtain a fuller participation in His victory by a more complete observance of the Christian Sabbath.

134. THE FOURTH COMMANDMENT

Sir. 3, 1–16 (Douay, 1–18)	Prv. 4, 1–5
Lk. 2, 41–51	Prv. 6, 20–24
Jn. 6, 35–40	Prv. 23, 22–25
	Sir. 7, 27–36 (Douay, 29–40)

Introduction: God our Father speaks to us through His living Word. In this Scripture reading He teaches us about the Fourth Commandment: "Honor your father and your mother." Let us be attentive as He tells us that we should honor our parents by constant obedience, just as Christ, our Lord, was obedient to His earthly parents and to His heavenly Father. In preparation for our reading let us recite Proverbs 4, verses 1–5.

First Reading: The Word of God as recorded in the Book of

Sirach, chapter 3, verses 1–16. In this reading God is telling us that we honor our parents by a loving and constant obedience.

℄ In grateful response to the Word we have received, let us recite Proverbs 6, verses 20–24.

Second Reading: The Word of God as recorded in the Gospel according to St. Luke, chapter 2, verses 41–51. In this reading God is telling us that Christ as a boy was obedient to His earthly parents.

℄ In grateful response to the Word we have received, let us recite Proverbs 23, verses 22–25.

Third Reading: The Word of God as recorded in the Gospel according to St. John, chapter 6, verses 35–40. In this reading God is telling us that Christ came down from heaven not to do His own will but the will of His heavenly Father.

℄ In grateful response to the Word we have received, let us recite Sirach 7, verses 27–36.

Conclusion: Let us thank God the Father for teaching us the Fourth Commandment and God the Son for showing us how to live it, and let us join in this prayer:

O God, Your Divine Son, Jesus Christ, has shown us the way of perfect obedience by always doing Your will; teach us, Your Chosen People, to honor and love our parents, and to be obedient and kind to our superiors.

135. THE FIFTH COMMANDMENT

Gn.	4, 1–16	Pss.	36, 1–15
2 Sm. (2 Kgs.)	12, 1–14		9b, 1–12
Mt.	14, 1–12		50, 1–11
			58, 2–11

Introduction: God our Father instructs us through His living Word. In this Scripture reading He teaches us the Fifth Commandment: "You shall not kill." Let us be attentive as He tells us how ugly the sin of murder is, with three examples from Holy Scripture: Cain murdered Abel; King David killed Urias, husband of Bathsheba; and Herod Antipas brutally murdered St. John the Baptist. In preparation for our reading let us recite Psalm 36, verses 1–15.

First Reading: The Word of God as recorded in the Book of Genesis, chapter 4, verses 1–16. In this reading God is telling us He was greatly displeased with Cain for the murder of his brother Abel.

¶ In response to the Word we have received, let us recite Psalm 9b, verses 1–12.

Second Reading: The Word of God as recorded in the Second Book of Samuel, chapter 12, verses 1–14. In this reading God is telling us that He punished David for the murder of Urias, husband of Bathsheba.

¶ In response to the Word we have received, let us recite Psalm 50, verses 1–11.

Third Reading: The Word of God as recorded in the Gospel according to St. Matthew, chapter 14, verses 1–12. In this reading God is telling us that Herod sinned against the Fifth Commandment when he commanded the head of John the Baptist brought in on a dish.

¶ In response to the Word we have received, let us recite Psalm 58, verses 2–11.

Conclusion: Let us give thanks to God for teaching us about the Fifth Commandment, and let us express our need for God's help by reciting this prayer:

Pardon, O Lord, the faults which Your people have committed out of human weakness; and may Your loving-kindness deliver us from the entanglements of sin.

136. THE SIXTH AND NINTH COMMANDMENTS

Sir.	23,	16–27	Pss.	105,	1–12
	(Douay,	21–38)		35,	2–10
Mt.	5,	27–30		140,	1–10
Gal.	5,	16–25		25,	1–8
1 Cor.	6,	13b–20	Sir.	22,	27–23, 6 (Douay 22, 33–23, 6)

Introduction: God, who rewards the just and punishes the evil, speaks to us through His living Word. In this Scripture reading He teaches us the Sixth and Ninth Commandments: "You shall not commit adultery. . . . You shall not covet your neighbor's wife." Let us be attentive as He tells us that sins of the flesh, whether in thought or in deed, are serious offenses; that we must be chaste and be led by the Spirit of God, whose temples we are. In preparation for our reading let us recite Psalm 105, verses 1–12.

First Reading: The Word of God as recorded in the Book of Sirach, chapter 23, verses 16–27. In this reading God is telling us that sins of the flesh are fires that will eventually devour the lustful man.

℄ In response to the Word we have received, let us recite Psalm 35, verses 2–10.

Second Reading: The Word of God as recorded in the Gospel according to St. Matthew, chapter 5, verses 27–30. In this reading God is telling us that lustful desires are a serious sin.

℄ In response to the Word we have received, let us recite Psalm 140, verses 1–10.

Third Reading: The Word of God as recorded in the Epistle to the Galatians, chapter 5, verses 16–25. In this reading God is telling us that to avoid impurity we must walk in the Spirit.

℄ In grateful response to the Word we have received, let us recite Psalm 25, verses 1–8.

Fourth Reading: The Word of God as recorded in the First Epistle to the Corinthians, chapter 6, verses 13b–20. In this reading God is giving us great motives for being pure: we are members of Christ, temples of the Holy Spirit, and redeemed for a great price.

℄ In grateful response to the Word we have received, let us recite Sirach 22, verse 27 to chapter 23, verse 6.

Conclusion: Let us express our deep thanks to God for His salutary teaching on the virtue of purity by reciting the following prayer:

O God, our protector and our guardian, come to our aid, and restore to our hearts and bodies the strength of purity and the freshness of chastity that, fed by the Body and Blood of Your Son, Jesus Christ, we may be cleansed from all temptations.

137. THE SEVENTH AND TENTH COMMANDMENTS

Lk. 19, 1–10	Is. 10, 1–4
Jn. 12, 1–8	Pss. 61, 10–13
Lk. 23, 39–43	40, 10–13
	53, 3–9

Introduction: God, who rewards the just and punishes the evil, speaks to us through His living Word. In this Scripture reading He communicates His teaching on the Seventh and Tenth Commandments: "You shall not steal. . . . You shall not covet your neighbor's goods." Let us be attentive as He shows us three examples which illustrate these commandments: Zacchaeus, Judas, and the thief upon the cross. In preparation for our reading let us recite Isaias 10, verses 1–4.

First Reading: The Word of God as recorded in the Gospel according to St. Luke, chapter 19, verses 1–10. In this reading God is telling us that Zacchaeus, a sinner, upon his conversion to Christ made a generous promise to return stolen money and give one-half of his possessions to the poor.

℄ In grateful response to the Word we have received, let us recite Psalm 61, verses 10–13.

Second Reading: The Word of God as recorded in the Gospel according to St. John, chapter 12, verses 1–8. In this reading God is telling us that Judas Iscariot, who betrayed Jesus, was a thief.

℄ In response to the Word we have received, let us recite Psalm 40, verses 10–13.

Third Reading: The Word of God as recorded in the Gospel according to St. Luke, chapter 23, verses 39–43. In this reading God is telling us that the thief on the cross repented and received the promise of paradise.

℄ In grateful response to the Word we have received, let us recite Psalm 53, verses 3–9.

Conclusion: Let us thank God for teaching us about the Seventh and Tenth Commandments, and let us ask God's mercy with this prayer:

O God, who punished Judas for his crime and rewarded the good thief for his faith, be merciful to us; and as our Lord Jesus Christ in His Passion gave to each of them what they deserved, so may He blot out our failings in the past and grant us a part in His Resurrection.

138. THE EIGHTH COMMANDMENT

Prv. 26, 18–28	Pss. 11, 2–9
Dn. 13, 42–63	51, 3–7
Mt. 26, 57–64	108, 1–5
	63, 2–11

Introduction: God, who rewards the just and punishes the evil, speaks to us through His living Word. In this Scripture reading He teaches us about the Eighth Commandment: "You shall not bear false witness against your neighbor." Let us be attentive as He tells us that bearing false witness is a serious sin against our neighbor; that one who lies does great harm and will not escape punishment; and that false witness was made against His own Son, Jesus Christ, at the time of His Passion. In preparation for our reading let us recite Psalm 11, verses 2–9.

First Reading: The Word of God as recorded in the Book of Proverbs, chapter 26, verses 18–28. In this reading God is telling us that one who bears false witness against another commits serious sin and is not to be trusted.

℄ In response to the Word we have received, let us recite Psalm 51, verses 3–7.

Second Reading: The Word of God as recorded in the Book of Daniel, chapter 13, verses 42–63. In this reading God is telling us that the elders bore false witness against Susanna; God punished them for their deceit.

℄ In response to the Word we have received, let us recite Psalm 108, verses 1–5.

Third Reading: The Word of God as recorded in the Gospel according to St. Matthew, chapter 26, verses 57–64. In this reading

God is telling us that false witness was brought against His own Son, Jesus Christ, at the time of His Passion.

◖ In response to the Word we have received, let us recite Psalm 63, verses 2–11.

Conclusion: Let us thank God for His teaching on the Eighth Commandment and let us recite this prayer:

Break for us, O Lord, the bonds of sin, and mercifully turn away from us the punishment we have deserved.

139. SIN

Gn.	3,	1–24	Prv.	1,	8–19	
Lk.	15,	11–32	Sir.	21,	1–5	(Douay, 1–6)
Lk.	5,	17–26	Sir.	17,	19–24	(20–28)
			Os.	6,	1–3	

Introduction: God, who rewards the just and punishes the evil, speaks to us through His living Word. In this Scripture reading He instructs us on sin. Let us be attentive as He tells us that sin has turned man away from Him; since God is a loving Father, however, He welcomes man back to Himself, and sends His beloved Son to forgive man's sins. In preparation for our reading let us recite Proverbs 1, verses 8–19.

First Reading: The Word of God as recorded in the Book of Genesis, chapter 3, verses 1–24. In this reading God is telling us that by sin our first parents turned away from their Maker.

◖ In response to the Word we have received, let us recite Sirach 21, verses 1–5.

Second Reading: The Word of God as recorded in the Gospel according to St. Luke, chapter 15, verses 11–32. In this reading God is telling us that He is a loving Father who welcomes sinful man back to Himself.

◖ In grateful response to the Word we have received, let us recite Sirach 17, verses 19–24.

Third Reading: The Word of God as recorded in the Gospel ac-

cording to St. Luke, chapter 5, verses 17–26. In this reading God is telling us that He sent His beloved Son to forgive man's sins.

❡ In grateful response to the Word we have received, let us recite Osee 6, verses 1–3.

Conclusion: Let us express our deep thanks to God for forgiving our sins, and let us make an Act of Contrition.

140. PRIDE

Gn. 11, 1–9	Is. 2, 10–17
Sir. 10, 6–18 (Douay, 6–22)	Is. 13, 9–12
Mt. 23, 1–28	Ps. 130, 1–3
	Lk. 1, 46–55

Introduction: God, who rewards the just and punishes the evil, speaks to us through His living Word. In this Scripture reading He communicates to us His teaching on the sin of pride. Let us be attentive as He tells us that, as at the Tower of Babel, He scatters the proud; that pride is hateful before God and men, and that Jesus denounced the Scribes and Pharisees for their pride. In preparation for our reading, let us recite Isaias 2, verses 10–17.

First Reading: The Word of God as recorded in the Book of Genesis, chapter 11, verses 1–9. In this reading God is telling us that He scatters the proud as He did in the parable of the Tower of Babel.

❡ In response to the Word we have received, let us recite Isaias 13, verses 9–12.

Second Reading: The Word of God as recorded in the Book of Sirach, chapter 10, verses 6–18. In this reading God is telling us that pride is hateful before God and men.

❡ In response to the Word we have received, let us recite Psalm 130, verses 1–3.

Third Reading: The Word of God as recorded in the Gospel according to St. Matthew, chapter 23, verses 1–28. In this reading

God is telling us that Jesus denounced the Scribes and Pharisees for their pride and hypocrisy.

¶ In response to the Word we have received, let us recite the Canticle of Mary from the Gospel according to St. Luke, chapter 1, verses 46–55.

Conclusion: Let us express our thanks to God for His teaching on the sin of pride, and let us ask Him to root out our pride as we recite this prayer:

O God, take away from us, we pray, that spirit of pride and arrogance which is so displeasing to You. Fill us with a spirit of fear, and give us a contrite and humble heart, that we may be enabled with pure minds to enter into the Holy of Holies.

141. ENVY

Gn.	37, 5–28		Sir.	30, 21–25
Nm.	12, 1–15		Pss.	104, 16–22
1 Sm. (1 Kgs.)	18, 5–16			77, 1–8
				36, 1–9

Introduction: God, who rewards the just and punishes the evil, speaks to us through His living Word. In this Scripture reading He teaches us about the sin of envy. Let us be attentive as He shows us three examples of envy: the envy of the sons of Jacob for their brother Joseph; the envy of Miriam and Aaron against Moses; and the envy of Saul against David. In all three cases God punished the sin. In preparation for our reading let us recite Sirach 30, verses 21–25.

First Reading: The Word of God as recorded in the Book of Genesis, chapter 37, verses 5–28. In this reading God is telling us that Joseph's brothers were so envious of him that they sold him to traders going to Egypt.

¶ In response to the Word we have received, let us recite Psalm 104, verses 16–22.

Second Reading: The Word of God as recorded in the Book of

Numbers, chapter 12, verses 1–15. In this reading God is telling us that He punished Miriam and Aaron for being envious of Moses.

¶ In response to the Word we have received, let us recite Psalm 77, verses 1–8.

Third Reading: The Word of God as recorded in First Book of Samuel, chapter 18, verses 5–16. In this reading God is telling us of the envy Saul had for David when the young warrior gained popular acclaim.

¶ In response to the Word we have received, let us recite Psalm 36, verses 1–9.

Conclusion: Let us thank God for warning us against the sin of envy, and let us recite this prayer:

O God, creator of all things, You have endowed every man with certain gifts according to Your divine plan; grant that we, Your humble creatures, may be satisfied with the gifts we have received, and always be thankful for them.

142. SLOTH

Prv.	6,	6–11	Pss.	127,	1–6
Mt.	25,	14–30		129,	1–8
2 Thes.	3,	6–15		50,	9–14
				31,	1–11

Introduction: God, who rewards and punishes the evil, speaks to us through His living Word. In this Scripture reading He teaches us about the sin of sloth. Let us be attentive as He tells us that we should take to heart the example of the industrious little ant — that we should avoid sloth and use our talents as best we can by working diligently for the good of all. In preparation for our reading let us recite Psalm 127, verses 1–6.

First Reading: The Word of God as recorded in the Book of Proverbs, chapter 6, verses 6–11. In this reading God is telling us that the example of the industrious little ant shows that sloth must be avoided.

◖ In grateful response to the Word we have received, let us recite Psalm 129, verses 1–8.

Second Reading: The Word of God as recorded in the Gospel according to St. Matthew, chapter 25, verses 14–30. In this reading God is telling us that we must guard against sloth and make use of the talents which He has given us.

◖ In response to the Word we have received, let us recite Psalm 50, verses 9–14.

Third Reading: The Word of God as recorded in the Second Epistle to the Thessalonians, chapter 3, verses 6–15. In this reading God is telling us not to give in to sloth, but to follow St. Paul's example by being diligent in doing good.

◖ In grateful response to the Word we have received, let us recite Psalm 31, verses 1–11.

Conclusion: Let us thank God for teaching us the evil of sloth and the need to do good, and let us recite this prayer:

Hear the prayers of Your Family, almighty God, and grant that by our frequent reception of the sacraments we may overcome our laziness and be dedicated to our work.

143. AN EVIL AND LYING TONGUE

Sir.	28,	12–26 (Douay, 14–30)	Prv.	4,	20–27
Mt.	7,	1–5	Pss.	139,	2–8
Jas.	3,	2–12		63,	2–11
				38,	1–9

Introduction: God, who rewards the just and punishes the evil, speaks to us through His living Word. In this Scripture reading He communicates to us His teaching on an evil tongue. Let us be attentive as He tells us that an evil tongue is the cause of great distress for others, that man is not to pass judgment on his fellow man at all, and that the man who can control his tongue can control his whole body. In preparation for our reading let us recite Proverbs 4, verses 20–27.

First Reading: The Word of God as recorded in Sirach, chapter 28, verses 12–26. In this reading God is telling us that an evil tongue is the cause of great distress for others.

℄ In response to the Word we have received, let us recite Psalm 139, verses 2–8.

Second Reading: The Word of God as recorded in the Gospel according to St. Matthew, chapter 7, verses 1–5. In this reading God is telling us through His Son that we should not judge our neighbor at all, lest a greater judgment befall us.

℄ In response to the Word we have received, let us recite Psalm 63, verses 2–11.

Third Reading: The Word of God as recorded in the Epistle of St. James, chapter 3, verses 2–12. In this reading God is telling us that the man who can control his tongue can control his whole body.

℄ In response to the Word we have received, let us recite Psalm 38, verses 1–9.

Conclusion: Let us express our thanks to God for this instruction on the evils of a treacherous tongue, and let us recite this prayer for the right use of our tongue:

Lord God, You have blessed us with the gift of speech that we might praise You and converse with one another; grant, we pray, that we may ever use this gift for the good of all men and for the glory of Your name.

144. DEATH

Gn.	3,	1–19	Eccl.	12,	1–7
Mt.	10,	23–28	Sir.	41,	1–4 (Douay, 1–7)
Ap.	21,	1–8	Ps.	114,	1–9
			Wis.	2,	23–3, 3

Introduction: God, who rewards the just and punishes the evil, speaks to us through His living Word. In this Scripture reading He teaches us about death. Let us be attentive as He tells us that there are two deaths: the first death is the death of the body and is the result of Adam's sin; the second is the death of the soul condemned to hell. For God's holy ones there shall be no second death. In preparation for our reading let us recite Ecclesiastes 12, verses 1–7.

First Reading: The Word of God as recorded in the Book of Genesis, chapter 3, verses 1–19. In this reading God is telling us that Adam and his sons must die because of sin. This is the first death.

℄ In response to the Word we have received, let us recite Sirach 41, verses 1–4.

Second Reading: The Word of God as recorded in the Gospel according to St. Matthew, chapter 10, verses 23–28. In this reading God is telling us that far worse than the first death is the death of the soul in hell.

℄ In response to the Word we have received, let us recite Psalm 114, verses 1–9.

Third Reading: The Word of God as recorded in the Apocalypse, chapter 21, verses 1–8. In this reading God is telling us that the wicked shall die a second death when their souls are condemned to hell. God's holy ones, on the other hand, will not undergo the second death, but will enjoy an eternal life of happiness.

℄ In response to the Word we have received, let us recite Wisdom, chapter 2, verse 23 to chapter 3, verse 3.

Conclusion: Let us express our deep thanks to God for His teaching on death and let us say this prayer for a happy death:

O God, grant us the grace of a happy death;
May the angels lead us to paradise;
May the martyrs welcome our arrival
  and lead us into the holy city of Jerusalem;
May the choir of angels receive us,
And with the once poor Lazarus may we enjoy an eternal rest.
Through Jesus Christ, Your Son and our Judge.
Amen.

145. THE RESURRECTION OF THE JUST

Lk.	20, 27–40	Jb.	19, 23–29
Jn.	11, 32–44	Pss.	72, 23–28
1 Cor.	15, 12–21		62, 2–9
			41, 2–6

Introduction: God our Father speaks to us through His living Word. In this Scripture reading He communicates to us His teaching on the resurrection of the just. Let us be attentive as He tells us that the dead shall rise, that the raising of Lazarus is a pledge of our own rising on the Last Day, and that the final resurrection is as certain as the very Resurrection of Jesus. In preparation for our reading let us recite Job 19, verses 23–29.

First Reading: The Word of God as recorded in the Gospel according to St. Luke, chapter 20, verses 27–40. In this reading God is telling us through His Son that the just will rise and will die no more.
¶ In grateful response to the Word we have received, let us recite Psalm 72, verses 23–28.

Second Reading: The Word of God as recorded in the Gospel according to St. John, chapter 11, verses 32–44. In this reading God is telling us that the resurrection of Lazarus is a pledge of our own resurrection on the Last Day.
¶ In grateful response to the Word we have received, let us recite Psalm 62, verses 2–9.

Third Reading: The Word of God as recorded in the First Epistle to the Corinthians, chapter 15, verses 12–21. In this reading God is telling us that the Resurrection of Christ is the assurance that we shall rise on the Last Day.
¶ In grateful response to the Word we have received, let us recite Psalm 41, verses 2–6.

Conclusion: Let us express our deep thanks to God for our hope in the resurrection on the Last Day by reciting this prayer:

O Lord, by the Passion, death, and Resurrection of Your Son, Jesus Christ, You have snatched us from the certainty of eternal death; grant us, we pray, the wonderful gift of joining in the resurrection of the just on the Last Day.

146. THE JUDGMENT OF THE LAST DAY

So.	1, 14–18		Pss.	49, 1–6
Mt.	25, 31–46			75, 2–10
1 Thes.	5, 1–11			74, 2–11
			Jl.	3, 9–16

Introduction: God, who rewards the just and punishes the evil, speaks to us through His living Word. In this Scripture reading He teaches us about the judgment of the Last Day. Let us be attentive as He tells us that the day of the Last Judgment will be a day of distress and gloom for the wicked; that the Son of Man, Jesus Christ, will be the judge who will separate the sheep from the goats for heaven or for hell; and that the day of the Lord will come without warning. In preparation for our reading let us recite Psalm 49, verses 1–6.

First Reading: The Word of God as recorded in the Book of Sophonias, chapter 1, verses 14–18. In this reading God is telling us that the great day of the Lord, a day of distress and darkness for the wicked, is near and speeding fast.

¶ In response to the Word we have received, let us recite Psalm 75, verses 2–10.

Second Reading: The Word of God as recorded in the Gospel according to St. Matthew, chapter 25, verses 31–46. In this reading God is telling us that Christ, the Son of Man and Judge on the Last Day, will separate the sheep from the goats for heaven or for hell.

¶ In response to the Word we have received, let us recite Psalm 74, verses 2–11.

Third Reading: The Word of God as recorded in the First Epistle to the Thessalonians, chapter 5, verses 1–11. In this reading God is telling us that we should be well prepared for the coming of our Judge, who shall come as a thief in the night.

¶ In response to the Word we have received, let us recite Joel 3, verses 9–16.

Conclusion: Let us thank God for this salutary teaching on the Last Judgment, and let us pray for a favorable verdict:

O God, the creator and redeemer of all the faithful, graciously forgive the sins of Your children, that through prayer and fasting we may obtain pardon for our sins and receive the reward of heaven on the Last Day.

147. CHRIST OUR JUDGE

Is.	11, 1–5	**Pss.**	9a, 2–11
Mt.	25, 1–13		25, 1–12
2 Tm.	4, 1–8	**Is.**	65, 8–14
		Is.	63, 1–6

Introduction: God, who rewards the just and punishes the evil, speaks to us through His living Word. In this Scripture reading He communicates to us His teaching on Christ our judge. Let us be attentive as He tells us that He will send us a judge who is just and merciful; and that we must be ever ready for the coming of this judge, Jesus Christ, who will pass sentence on the living and the dead at the end of time. In preparation for our reading let us recite Psalm 9a, verses 2–11.

First Reading: The Word of God as recorded in the Book of Isaias, chapter 11, verses 1–5. In this reading God is telling us that He will send us a judge who is just and merciful.

℄ In grateful response to the Word we have received, let us recite Psalm 25, verses 1–12.

Second Reading: The Word of God as recorded in the Gospel according to St. Matthew, chapter 25, verses 1–13. In this reading God is telling us, through the parable of the Ten Virgins, that we must always be prepared for this great Judge who is to come.

℄ In grateful response to the Word we have received, let us recite Isaias 65, verses 8–14.

Third Reading: The Word of God as recorded in the Second Epistle to Timothy, chapter 4, verses 1–8. In this reading God is telling us that this great judge is His beloved Son, Jesus Christ, who will judge us according to our deeds at the end of the world.

℄ In grateful response to the Word we have received, let us recite Isaias 63, verses 1–6.

Conclusion: Let us express our thanks to God for Christ, our just and merciful judge, by reciting this prayer:

O God, You know that it is because of our sins that we are rightly saddened; grant that we may be consoled by the coming of Jesus Christ, our just and merciful judge.

148. HEAVEN

Jn. 14, 1–4	Wis. 3, 1–9	
Mt. 25, 14–23	Pss. 121, 1–9	
Ap. 22, 1–5	46, 2–10	
	26, 1–6	

Introduction: God, who rewards the just and punishes the evil, speaks to us through His living Word. In this Scripture reading He teaches us about heaven. Let us be attentive as He tells us that heaven is our Father's house which Jesus has made ready for us; that it can be entered only by using rightly all the gifts that God has given us; and that it is the throne-city of God, where the just shall rejoice before the Face of God forever. In preparation for our reading let us recite Wisdom 3, verses 1–9.

First Reading: The Word of God as recorded in the Gospel according to St. John, chapter 14, verses 1–4. In this reading God is telling us that heaven is our true home, the house of our Father which Jesus has made ready for us.

℄ In grateful response to the Word we have received, let us recite Psalm 121, verses 1–9.

Second Reading: The Word of God as recorded in the Gospel according to St. Matthew, chapter 25, verses 14–23. In this reading God is telling us, through the parable of the Talents, that we must win heaven by using correctly all the gifts He has given us.

℄ In grateful response to the Word we have received, let us recite Psalm 46, verses 2–10.

Third Reading: The Word of God as recorded in the Apocalypse, chapter 22, verses 1–5. In this reading God is telling us that heaven is the throne-city of God, where the just shall rejoice in seeing God for ever and ever.

℄ In grateful response to the Word we have received, let us recite Psalm 26, verses 1–6.

Conclusion: Let us express our deep thanks to God for His teaching on heaven by reciting this prayer:

Lord God of salvation, You sent Your Son, the Lamb of God, to redeem man by His blood and open the gates to paradise; may we, Your Chosen People, share in His redemption by our frequent reception of the Eucharist, and thereby prepare for seeing You face to face in heaven.

149. HELL

Mt. 13, 24–30 & 36-43		Hb. 3, 2–15
Mt. 25, 31–46		Is. 47, 14–15
Lk. 16, 19–31		Is. 33, 10–14
		Is. 9, 18–21

Introduction: God, who rewards the just and punishes the evil, speaks to us through His living Word. In this Scripture reading He communicates to us His teaching on hell. Let us be attentive as He tells us that a wicked life on earth will receive its just punishment when the Son of Man will condemn the sinner to the fires of hell. In preparation for our reading let us recite Habacuc 3, verses 2–15.

First Reading: The Word of God as recorded in the Gospel according to St. Matthew, chapter 13, verses 24–30 and 36–43. In this reading God is telling us, through the parable of the Weeds, that those who live wicked lives on earth will receive a just punishment after death.

℄ In response to the Word we have received, let us recite Isaias 47, verses 14–15.

Second Reading: The Word of God as recorded in the Gospel according to St. Matthew, chapter 25, verses 31–46. In this reading God is telling us that in the Judgment the Son of Man will condemn the wicked into the everlasting fire of hell.

◖ In response to the Word we have received, let us recite Isaias 33, verses 10–14.

Third Reading: The Word of God as recorded in the Gospel according to St. Luke, chapter 16, verses 19–31. In this reading God is telling us through the parable of Lazarus and the Rich Man that the wicked, once condemned by God in the Judgment, will never be able to escape the torments of hell.

◖ In response to the Word we have received, let us recite Isaias 9, verses 18–21.

Conclusion: Let us express our deep thanks to God for His warning about hell, and let us recite this prayer:

O God, judge of mankind, who rewarded Lazarus with heaven and buried the rich man in hell, give to us, Your People, a sincere sorrow for sin, that by our penance and prayers we may avoid the punishment of hell-fire and obtain the reward of heaven.

150. CHRIST IN HIS GLORY

Lk.	9, 28–36		Is.	64,	1–4
Acts	1, 1–11		Pss.	28,	1–11
Mt.	24, 23–31			46,	2–10
			Jl.	3,	14–21

Introduction: In Sacred Scripture God is ever telling us of His Divine Word. In this Scripture reading He communicates to us His teaching on the glory of Christ. Let us be attentive as He tells us that at the Transfiguration Christ showed His glory to three of His apostles; at His Ascension Christ showed His glory to many disciples; and at the end of the world Christ will show His glory to all the tribes of the earth. In preparation for our reading let us recite Isaias 64, verses 1–4.

First Reading: The Word of God as recorded in the Gospel according to St. Luke, chapter 9, verses 28–36. In this reading God is telling us that Peter, James, and John were witnesses to Christ's brilliant Transfiguration.

¶ In grateful response to the Word we have received, let us recite Psalm 28, verses 1–11.

Second Reading: The Word of God as recorded in the Acts of the Apostles, chapter 1, verses 1–11. In this reading God is telling us that many of the disciples witnessed Christ's glorious Ascension.

¶ In grateful response to the Word we have received, let us recite Psalm 46, verses 2–10.

Third Reading: The Word of God as recorded in the Gospel according to St. Matthew, chapter 24, verses 23–31. In this reading God is telling us that all the tribes of the earth will be witnesses to Christ's splendid Second Coming at the end of the world.

¶ In joyful response to the Word we have received, let us recite Joel 3, verses 14–21.

Conclusion: Let us express our deep thanks to God for teaching us about Christ in His glory and let us recite this prayer:

O Lord Jesus Christ, Saviour and Judge,
Come and stand in the midst of us;
Receive us into Your glory;
Give us lasting peace.
Come, Lord Jesus!
MaránaTha
Come!

APPENDIX A
Additional Bible Readings

1a. God, Creator and Keeper of the Universe
Sir. 39, 12–35 (Douay, 16–41)
Sir. 42, 15–25 (15–26)
Sir. 43, 1–35 (1–37)

1b. The Wisdom and Power of God in Creation
Jb. 38
Jb. 39
Jb. 40
Jb. 41

2a. Noe
Gn. 6, 9–22
Gn. 7, 1–24
Gn. 8, 1–22
Gn. 9, 1–17

5a. The Sin and Punishment of Sodom and Gomorra
Gn. 18, 16–33
Gn. 19, 1–14
Gn. 19, 15–29

5b. A Wife for Isaac
Gn. 24, 1–28
Gn. 24, 29–49
Gn. 24, 50–67

5c. Jacob Receives His Father's Blessing
Gn. 27, 1–13
Gn. 27, 14–29
Gn. 27, 30–40

5d. Jacob and Rachel
Gn. 29, 1–35
Gn. 30, 1–43
Gn. 31, 1–24
Gn. 31, 25–32, 3

7a. Moses as Leader
Ex. 2, 1–15
Ex. 2, 23–3, 15
Ex. 14, 10–31

7b. The Ten Plagues
Ex. 7, 14–8, 11
Ex. 8, 12–9, 12
Ex. 9, 13–10, 20
Ex. 10, 21–11, 10

7c. The Providence of God in the Exodus
Wis. 16
Wis. 17
Wis. 18
Wis. 19

8a. Moses as Lawgiver
Sir. 45, 1–5 (Douay, 1–6)
Ex. 34, 17–35
Dt. 5, 22–6, 9

18a. Josue
Sir. 46, 1–8 (Douay, 1–10)
Jos. 3, 1–17
Jos. 8, 1–23
Jos. 24, 19–28

23a. David Slays Goliath
1 Sm. (1 Kgs.) 17, 1–19
1 Sm. (1 Kgs.) 17, 20–40
1 Sm. (1 Kgs.) 17, 41–58

24a. The Wisdom of Solomon
Wis. 8, 17–9, 18
3 Kgs. 3, 16–28
3 Kgs. 10, 1–13

27a. Ezechias
Sir. 48, 17–25 (Douay, 19–38)
2 Chron. (2 Par.) 32, 1–23
4 Kgs. 20, 1–11
4 Kgs. 20, 12–21

27b. From Second and Third Isaias
Is. 43, 1–13
Is. 54, 7–14
Is. 61, 1–11

27c. Servant of the Lord Poems
Is. 42, 1–9
Is. 49, 1–6
Is. 50, 4–11
Is. 52, 13–53, 12

28a. Josias
Sir. 49, 1–7 (Douay, 1–9)
2 Chron. (2 Par.) 34, 1–13
2 Chron. (2 Par.) 34, 14–33
2 Chron. (2 Par.) 35, 20–27

29a. From the Book of Lamentations
Lam. 2, 1–22
Lam. 4, 1–22
Lam. 5, 1–22

30a. The Restoration in Ezechiel
Ez. 36, 22–28
Ez. 37, 1–14
Ez. 47, 1–12

36a. Angels in the Old Testament
Jgs. 13, 1–25
Tb. 5, 1–21
Is. 6, 1–7

36b. Angels in the New Testament
Mt. 28, 1–7
Acts 12, 6–11
Ap. 7, 1–12

36c. Gabriel the Archangel
Dn. 9, 20–27
Lk. 1, 5–25
Lk. 1, 26–38

38a. The Birth of St. John the Baptist
Mal. 4, 1–6
Lk. 1, 5–25
Lk. 1, 39–47
Lk. 1, 57–80

39a. The Presentation of Jesus and the Purification of Mary
Gn. 17, 1–14
Lv. 12, 1–8
Lk. 2, 21–40

39b. The Finding in the Temple
Mal. 3, 1–5
Lk. 2, 41–52
Mk. 11, 15–18

40a. Call of the Gentiles
Is. 2, 1–4
Mk. 7, 24–30
Jn. 4, 1–45
Acts 10, 1–33

40b. Parables on the Rejection of the Jews and the Call of the Gentiles
Mk. 12, 1–12
Mt. 20, 1–16
Mt. 22, 1–14

42a. St. John the Baptist
Sir. 48, 4–12a Douay, 4–13a)
Mt. 17, 9–13
Mk. 6, 14–29

42b. The Desert
Ex. 15, 22–16, 3
Lk. 3, 1–18
Lk. 4, 1–13

45a. The Apostles before the Resurrection
Lk. 6, 12–16
Lk. 9, 1–11
Mt. 26, 47–56

45b. The Apostles after the Resurrection
1 Cor. 15, 1–8
Acts 1, 15–26
Acts 15, 1–31

45c. The Apostles, Fishers of Men
Mk. 1, 14–20
Lk. 5, 1–11
Jn. 21, 1–14

48a. Christ's Power over the Devil
Lk. 4, 1–13
Lk. 8, 26–39
Lk. 9, 37–44a

48b. Christ's Power over Sickness and Death
3 Kgs. 17, 17–24
Jer. 30, 12–17
Mt. 9, 18–26
Acts 9, 31–43

48c. Christ's Power over Blindness
Tb. 11, 1–16
Mt. 9, 27–31
Jn. 9, 1–11

51a. Christ, Divine Teacher
Jl. 2, 23–27
Lk. 4, 14–32
Mk. 4, 1–25

55a. Light and Darkness
Jn. 3, 16–21
1 Jn. 1, 5–2, 2
Ap. 21, 22–27

56a. Christ, Life-giver
4 Kgs. 4, 8–37
Jn. 4, 46–53
Acts 20, 7–12

60a. Christ our Mediator
Heb. 8, 1–6
Heb. 9, 11–15
Heb. 12, 18–24

65a. Jesus Christ, Son of David
Ps. 88, 20–30
1 Chron. (1 Par.) 17, 1–15
Jer. 23, 1–8
Mk. 10, 46–52

65b. Christ, the Son of Man
Dn. 7, 13–14
Mk. 8, 27–39
Mt. 24, 27–31
Ap. 1, 12–18

72a. The Trial of Jesus
Jn. 18, 12–24
Mt. 26, 57–68
Lk. 23, 1–25

75a. Death, Burial and Resurrection with Christ
Mk. 15, 37–16, 8
Rom. 6, 3–11
Eph. 5, 1–20

77a. The Ascension
Mk. 16, 14–20
Heb. 7, 26–8, 3
Eph. 2, 4–10

78a. Promise of the Holy Spirit
Jn. 14, 15–21
Jn. 16, 5–11
Jn. 16, 12–16

78b. The Holy Trinity
Rom. 11, 33–36
Lk. 3, 15–22
Mt. 28, 16–20
1 Jn. 5, 1–13

79a. The Church, the Family of Abraham
Gn. 21, 1–21
Jn. 8, 31–47
Gal. 4, 21–31

83a. The Kingdom of the Poor
Lk. 2, 8–20
Mt. 5, 1–12
Jas. 2, 1–13

84a. Jerusalem of Old
Mk. 10, 32–34
Lk. 13, 31–35
Lk. 19, 29–44
Lk. 21, 20–24

89a. The Church as the Remnant
Jer. 31, 7–14
Mt. 22, 1–14
Rom. 11, 5–22

91a. Three Gospel Miracles Symbolizing Baptism
Mk. 7, 31–37
Mk. 8, 22–26
Jn. 5, 1–15

95a. Jesus' Discourse on the Eucharist
Jn. 6, 22–34
Jn. 6, 35–48
Jn. 6, 49–59 (Greek, 49–58)
Jn. 6, 60–72 (Greek, 59–71)

101a. Deacons
1 Tm. 3, 8–13
Acts 6, 1–7
Acts 6, 8–15; 7, 54–60
Acts 8, 4–8; 8, 26–40

106a. St. Joseph
Ps. 111, 1–9
Mt. 1, 18–25
Mt. 2, 13–23

112a. St. Paul's Mission
Gal. 1, 11–24
Gal. 2, 1–10
Gal. 2, 11–20

113a. St. James, Son of Zebedee
Mk. 5, 35–43
Mk. 9, 1–7
Mt. 26, 36–46

118a. Conversion from Vice to Virtue
Jer. 3, 14–4, 4
1 Thes. 4, 1–12
Col. 3, 5–17
Jn. 8, 1–11

120a. The Power of Prayer
Is. 38, 1–6
Mt. 7, 7–11
Lk. 7, 1–10

122a. Fasting
Is. 58, 1–9a
Mk. 9, 13–28
2 Cor. 4, 7–18

125a. Men and Women of Faith
Heb. 11, 1–12
Heb. 11, 13–22
Heb. 11, 23–40

128a. Friendship
Sir. 6, 5–17
Sir. 11, 29–12, 18 (Douay, 11, 31–12, 19)
Sir. 22, 19–26 (Douay, 22, 24–32)

128b. Fraternal Charity
Lk. 6, 27–38
Mt. 18, 21–35
Rom. 12, 9–21

128c. Almsgiving
Dt. 15, 1–11
Mt. 6, 1–4
Mk. 12, 41–44
2 Cor. 9, 1–15

130a. Obedience
Gn. 22, 1–19
Mt. 2, 13–23
Col. 3, 18–24

131a. The Ten Commandments
Ex. 20, 1–17
Dt. 5, 1–21
Mk. 10, 17–27
Mk. 12, 28–34

133a. True Sabbath Observance
Is. 58, 13–14
Lk. 13, 10–17
Lk. 14, 1–6
Lk. 6, 1–11

139a. The Devil
Jb. 1, 1–2, 10
Mt. 9, 32–10, 10
1 Pt. 5, 5–11
Ap. 12, 7–12

139b. Temptation
Gn. 3, 1–13
Mt. 4, 1–11
1 Cor. 10, 1–13
Eph. 6, 10–17

141a. Anger
1 Sm. (1 Kgs.) 18, 6–12
Lk. 4, 16–30
Mt. 5, 21–26

141b. Avarice
Eccl. 5, 9–16
3 Kgs. 21, 1–19
Lk. 12, 13–21

142a. Scandal
2 Chron. (2 Par.) 33, 1–9
Mt. 18, 5–14
Rom. 14, 12–23

146a. The Coming Judgment
Gn. 7, 5–24
Gn. 19, 15–25
Lk. 17, 20–37

148a. Heaven
Is. 60, 1–22
2 Cor. 5, 1–10
Ap. 4, 1–11

150a. The Final Coming of Christ
Is. 66, 15–24
Mk. 13, 21–37
1 Thes. 4, 13–5, 11
2 Pt. 3, 8–13

APPENDIX B
Suggested Readings for the Liturgical Year

Temporal Cycle

Advent
- First Sunday, 41, 146*
- Second Sunday, 42, 126
- Third Sunday, 42a, 150a
  - Ember Wednesday, 105
  - Ember Friday, 107
  - Ember Saturday, 46
- Fourth Sunday, 27, 27b, 42b

Christmas
- Vigil, 106
- Christmas, 39, 52, 66, 126, 83a
- St. Stephen, 114
- St. John, 113
- Holy Innocents, 35
- St. Thomas of Canterbury, 58
- St. Sylvester, 110
- Sunday after Christmas, 52
- Circumcision, 106, 39a
- Holy Name, 18, 63, 64, 18a

Epiphany
- Epiphany, 40, 55, 148a
- Holy Family, 106, 134, 39b, 106a
- First Sunday, 67, 84
- Baptism of Christ, 43, 53
- Second Sunday, 104, 108
- Third Sunday, 47, 100
- Fourth Sunday, 86, 131a
- Fifth Sunday, 149, 118a
- Sixth Sunday, 146

Septuagesima
- Septuagesima Sunday, 1, 2, 3, 50, 57, 89, 40b
- Sexagesima Sunday, 119, 2a
- Quinquagesima Sunday, 4, 5, 118, 128, 5a, 65a, 125a

Lent
- Ash Wednesday, 122, 144
  - Thursday, 100, 120a
  - Friday, 122a, 128c
  - Saturday, 48, 133
- First Sunday, 44, 5b, 139b
  - Monday, 58, 146
  - Tuesday, 52, 119
  - Ember Wednesday, 9, 75
  - Thursday, 40a
  - Ember Friday, 91a
  - Ember Saturday, 150, 65b
- Second Sunday, 49, 62, 5c, 5d, 118a
  - Monday, 36, 74
  - Tuesday, 25, 140
  - Wednesday, 117, 84a
  - Thursday, 149
  - Friday, 6, 89, 40b
  - Saturday, 69, 139, 5c
- Third Sunday, 6, 136, 48a
  - Monday, 47
  - Tuesday, 26, 121
  - Wednesday, 17, 134, 131a
  - Thursday, 46
  - Friday, 57, 40a
  - Saturday, 138, 118a
- Fourth Sunday, 7, 51, 60, 95, 7a, 7b, 8a, 79a
  - Monday, 24, 54, 24a
  - Tuesday, 8

* Numbers refer to readings, not to pages.

Wednesday, 27, 55, 30a, 48c
Thursday, 56, 56a
Friday, 145, 48b
Saturday, 55, 58, 55a
Passiontide, 28, 29
Passion Sunday, 12, 37, 60a
Monday, 57, 122
Tuesday, 131
Wednesday, 128
Thursday, 68, 97
Friday, 29a
Saturday, 27c
Palm Sunday, 65, 129
Monday, 73
Tuesday, 53, 72a
Wednesday, 68, 72
Holy Thursday, 38, 96, 102, 95a
Good Friday, 14, 74
Easter
Vigil, 7, 55, 91
Easter Sunday, 3, 75, 75a
Monday, 76, 111
Tuesday, 73, 96, 112
Wednesday, 82, 95, 45c
Thursday, 43, 92, 117, 7c, 45b, 101a
Friday, 81, 114, 2a
Saturday, 80, 91
Low Sunday, 7, 66, 98, 125
Second Sunday, 58, 79, 123
Third Sunday, 16, 150
Fourth Sunday, 78a
Fifth Sunday, 119, 121
Rogation Days, 120
Vigil of Ascension, 85
Ascension Thursday, 77, 77a
Novena to the Holy Spirit
Friday, 1
Saturday, 78a
Sunday, 15
Monday, 78
Tuesday, 85
Wednesday, 93
Thursday, 94
Friday, 127
Saturday, 128
Sunday after the Ascension, 93
Pentecost
Vigil, 94, 78a
Pentecost, 8, 78
Monday, 111, 55a
Tuesday, 58, 93
Ember Wednesday, 15, 95
Thursday, 100, 101a
Ember Friday, 139, 51a
Ember Saturday, 36, 101, 102
Trinity Sunday, 78b
First Sunday, 127
Corpus Christi, 95, 96, 95a
Second Sunday, 83, 130
Sacred Heart, 53, 70
Third Sunday, 69, 139a
Fourth Sunday, 23a, 45c
Fifth Sunday, 135, 141a
Sixth Sunday, 95, 75a
Seventh Sunday, 119, 144, 24a
Eighth Sunday, 24
Ninth Sunday, 84a, 139b
Tenth Sunday, 120, 129
Eleventh Sunday, 45a, 91a
Twelfth Sunday, 99, 118
Thirteenth Sunday, 4, 47
Fourteenth Sunday, 126, 136
Fifteenth Sunday, 56, 124
Sixteenth Sunday, 129, 133a
Seventeenth Sunday, 23, 65, 85, 131a
Ember Wednesday, 13, 122a
Ember Friday, 97
Ember Saturday, 12, 133a
Eighteenth Sunday, 97
Nineteenth Sunday, 87, 40b, 89a
Twentieth Sunday, 56a, 75a
Twenty-first Sunday, 128b, 139b
Twenty-second Sunday, 71, 147
Twenty-third Sunday, 66, 148, 48b
Twenty-fourth Sunday, 29, 150, 65b, 146a

Sanctoral Cycle

December
8. Immaculate Conception, 105, 107
January
18. St. Peter's Chair at Rome, 110
25. Conversion of St. Paul, 112, 112a
February
2. Purification of Mary, 39a
22. St. Peter's Chair at Antioch, 111
March
19. St. Joseph, 106a
24. Gabriel the Archangel, 36c
25. Annunciation, 39, 105
May
1. St. Joseph the Worker, 124
3. Finding of the Holy Cross, 74

June
- 24. Nativity of St. John the Baptist, 42, 38a
- 29. Sts. Peter and Paul, 109
- 30. Commemoration of St. Paul, 112, 112a

July
- 1. Precious Blood, 12, 37
- 2. Visitation, 107
- 25. St. James, Son of Zebedee, 113a

August
- 1. St. Peter in Chains, 109
- 3. St. Stephen, 101a
- 5. Dedication of St. Mary Major, 106
- 6. Transfiguration, 9, 49, 150
- 15. Assumption, 108, 145
- 29. Beheading of St. John the Baptist, 42a

September
- Labor Day, 124
- 8. Nativity of the Blessed Virgin, 105
- 14. Exaltation of the Holy Cross, 74
- 15. Sorrowful Mother, 29a

October
- 11. Maternity of the Blessed Virgin, 39, 106
- Last Sunday. Christ the King, 59

November
- 1. All Saints, 53, 118, 83a
- 2. All Souls, 144
- 9. Dedication of St. John Lateran, 84
- 18. Dedication of the Basilicas of Sts. Peter and Paul, 90

Other Occasions

May and October Devotions

Joyful Mysteries
- First, 105
- Second, 107
- Third, 39
- Fourth, 39a
- Fifth, 39b

Sorrowful Mysteries
- First, 29a
- Second, 72, 72a
- Third, 28, 59
- Fourth, 73
- Fifth, 12, 14, 50, 74, 101, 106, 108

Glorious Mysteries
- First, 75, 76, 75a
- Second, 77, 77a
- Third, 15, 78, 78a
- Fourth, 145
- Fifth, 107

A Holy Hour in Honor of the Blessed Sacrament

Introduction: Ps. 135, 1–26

Readings:	Responses
Ex. 12, 21–28	Pss. 134, 1–9
Ex. 16, 1–15	94, 1–7
Jn. 6, 1–15	22, 1–6
Lk. 22, 14–20	115, 1–10
1 Cor. 11, 23–29	110, 1–5
Ap. 19, 6–10	99, 1–5

APPENDIX C
Suggestions for the Group-Use of This Book

The varying needs of individual groups will, of course, dictate the actual manner in which this book is used. For this reason, the suggestions which follow are of the most general nature, calculated to give a broad outline rather than a fixed format.

There should be, whenever possible, a lectern for the readers; upon it will rest the Holy Book. The Bible itself should be of the finest edition available to the group, so that the physical dignity of the book will emphasize the respect due to its contents. The leader does not read from the lectern, but from another suitable place.

It is most important that the readers prepare their respective passages beforehand, not only in order that they might be able to read the Bible slowly, intelligently and reverently, but also so that they might be better able to emphasize the theme which a given reading is meant to elucidate.

If the place where the readings are held permits, there should be a procession of the Book, that is, while all stand, the leader and the readers enter; the Book is carried by one of the members of the procession, much as is done by the deacon at the Gospel procession at solemn high Mass. As the procession enters, the group sings or recites an introductory hymn or Psalm. When the Psalm is finished, all sit, while the leader reads the Introduction, omitting the last sentence, "In preparation for our reading . . ."

If such a procession is not feasible, the opening Psalm is recited after the leader reads the Introduction. The Psalms, by the way, may be recited in unison, alternating between the leader and the group, or between two halves of the group. In the event that Bibles or Psalters are not available for the group, the leader may give the people a refrain (for example, "In verdant pastures He gives me repose" for Psalm 22). In any event, the group should stand until the opening Psalm has been completed.

The opening Psalm having been completed, the leader introduces the first reading. For each of the readings, the designated reader leaves his place and goes to the lectern. When the reading is completed, he returns to his place. The leader, if properly conversant with the material, may follow each reading with a short commentary on the passage; this commentary should not be more than three minutes in length. After the commentary, or after the reading itself if the former is not given, the leader invites the group to respond to the Word of God with a Psalm or hymn.

After the last Psalm has been sung, the group remains standing, while the leader offers the concluding prayer. Endings for these prayers may be found in Appendix D.

The question of substitution will be up to the leader or to the group itself. For instance, a hymn might be sung in place of the concluding prayer. Again, if it is not possible for all members of the group to have a Bible, but a Psalter only, it will be necessary to substitute suitable Psalms for the various responsories in the text which call for texts from other parts of the Bible. In fine, the "rubrics" of this exercise will depend primarily on the requirements of the group itself, if the readings are held within a group.

Following the conclusion of the reading, it would be not only appropriate but most desirable that the lesson inculcated by the reading be further illustrated by an action which will also serve to complete the reception of the Word by a concrete response. If the Bible reading is done in Church the action may be Benediction, or something from the Ritual such as the distribution of ashes on Ash Wednesday, or the blessing of throats on St. Blaise's Day or the distribution of candles on Candlemas Day, and so on. A recessional hymn or Psalm should then be used to terminate the ceremony.

The following is a rubrical outline of a typical reading, using unit 1, page 21, *above*.

Introduction: The group is seated. The leader stands from his place and reads, "God our Father speaks to us, . . . Psalm 148, verses 1–4." All recite the Psalm.

First Reading: The leader stands from his place and reads, "The Word of God . . . plants on the land." Meanwhile the first reader goes to the lectern. When the leader has finished, the first reader reads Genesis 1, 1–13.

℄ The leader reads, "In grateful response . . . verses 1–9," while the first reader returns to his place. All recite the Psalm.

Second Reading: The leader stands from his place and reads, "The Word of God . . . and the birds." Meanwhile the second reader goes to the lectern. When the leader has finished, the second reader reads Genesis 1, 14–23.

℄ The leader reads, "In grateful response . . . verses 2–7," while the second reader returns to his place. All recite the Psalm.

Third Reading: The leader stands from his place and reads, "The Word of God . . . on the seventh day." Meanwhile the third reader goes to the lectern. When the leader has finished, the third reader reads Genesis 1, 24–2, 3.

℄ The leaders reads, "In grateful response . . . verses 2–10," while the third reader returns to his place. All recite the Psalm.

Conclusion: All stand. The leader reads, "Let us express . . . the Our Father." All recite the Our Father.

APPENDIX D
Conclusions for Final Prayers

1. Through (Jesus) Christ, our Lord. Amen.
2. Through the same (Jesus) Christ, our Lord. Amen.
3. We pray this through our Lord Jesus Christ. Amen.
4. Through Your Son, our Lord Jesus Christ, who lives and reigns with You in the unity of the (same) Holy Spirit, God forever and ever. Amen.
5. Through (the same) Christ our Lord, who will come to judge the living and the dead, and the world by fire. Amen.
6. Through the power of (the same) Jesus Christ our Lord, who will come to judge the living and the dead and the world by fire. Amen.
7. Through Your Son, our Lord Jesus Christ, who comes from heaven as Bread, gives life and salvation to the world, and who lives and reigns together with the Holy Spirit, one God forever and ever. Amen.
8. Who live(s) and reign(s) forever and ever. Amen.
9. Who live(s) and reign(s) in the all-perfect Trinity, God forever and ever. Amen.
10. Who live(s) and reign(s) with God the Father in the unity of the (same) Holy Spirit, God forever and ever. Amen.

INDEX

This Index has been conceived of as a supplementary aid to the use of this book. Where possible, duplication of the Table of Contents has been avoided. Numbers refer to the units in the body of this volume.

Aaron, 10, 11, 101, 141
Abel, 135
Abraham, 4, 5, 38, 125
Adam, 1, 2, 50, 108, 144
Agony in the Garden, 121
Angels, 7, 14, 39, 59, 66
Anointing, 78, 99, 100
Apostles, 45, 61, 77, 81, 82, 86, 98, 100, 111, 123
Apostolicity of the Church, 82
Appearances of Jesus, 76
Ark of Noe, 86
Ark of the Covenant, 84, 107
Ascension, 76, 77, 150
Atonement, feast of, 12

Babel, Tower of, 94, 140
Baptism, 43, 57, 62, 91, 92
Bartimeus, 118
Bathsheba, 135
Bethlehem, 20, 40, 106
Blindness, 68
Blood of animals, 12, 37
Blood of Christ, 12, 37, 38
Boas, 20
Brazen serpent, 74, 99

Cain, 135
Cana, 104, 108
Catholicity of the Church, 81
Charity, 70, 87, 125, 127, 128
Chastity, 136
Chosen People, 4, 8, 16, 19
Christ, the name, 64
Church, *see* Table of Contents
Commandments, 17, 131, 132, 133, 134, 135, 136, 137, 138
Confessors, 115
Confirmation, 93, 94
Covenant, New, 37, 38
Covenant, Old, 5, 8, 37, 38
Covetousness, 137
Creation, 1, 2
Cross, Jesus lifted up on, 14, 74
Crucifixion, 62, 108, 129
Cyrus, 31

Daniel, 36, 131
David, 20, 21, 23, 24, 65, 78, 107, 135, 141
Death, 144
Death of Jesus, 50, 62

Egypt, Israel and, 4, 6, 7
Eleazar, 10, 123
Elias, 25, 26, 49, 55
Eliseus, 26, 47
Elizabeth, 107

Emmaus, 76
End of the world, 52, 145, 150
Envy, 141
Epiphany, 40
Esdras, 32
Esther, 117
Eucharist, 95, 96
Eve, 1, 2, 108
Evil tongue, 143
Example, good, 41, 123
Exile, 13, 30, 32, 33
Extreme unction, 99, 100
Ezechiel, 30, 58

Faith, 4, 125
False teachers, 52
False witness, 138
Fasting, 122
Fidelity, 17, 18, 33, 35, 36
Flood, 2

Gedeon, 19
Glory, 150
Goliath, 23
Good News, 41
Good Samaritan, 99, 118
Good Shepherd, 58, 69
Good thief, 68, 137

Heaven, 148
Hell, 149
Herod Antipas, 135
Holiness of the Church, 80
Holy People, Church, 11
Holy Spirit, 13, 15, 78, 92, 93, 94
Hope, 126
Humility, 129

Idolatry, 8, 36, 131
Isaias, 27, 39, 59, 81, 106
Israel, at Sinai, 8

Jacob, 4
James, son of Zebedee, 49
Jephte, 19
Jeremias, 28, 29, 73
Jericho, 18
Jerusalem, 29, 31, 32, 33, 84
Jesus Christ, *passim*. *See also* Table of Contents
Jesus, name, 63
John the Baptist, St., 42, 92, 135
John the Evangelist, St., 49, 93, 113
Jonas, 75
Jordan River, 18, 43, 62, 93
Joseph, 4, 6, 141
Joseph, St., 39
Josue, 16, 45, 63
Judas Iscariot, 137
Judas Machabeus, 34
Judges, 19
Judgment Day, 35, 40, 115, 146
Judith, 117
Justice, 71, 147

Lamb of God, 14, 53, 87
Last Supper, 14, 15, 96, 102
Lazarus, 46, 56, 145
Leprosy, 47
Life-giver, 56
Light of the World, 55
Lying, 138, 143

Machabees, 34, 35, 114
Magi, 40
Manifestations of God, 49
Martyrs, 114
Mary Magdalene, 117
Mary the Virgin, 39, 50, 59, 83, 105, 106, 107, 113, 116
Mathathias, 34
Matrimony, 103, 104
Melchisedech, 102
Mercy, 68, 122, 147
Messias, 64, 66, 67, 73, 106
Miriam, 141
Moses, 7, 8, 9, 16, 38, 49, 51, 60, 86, 120, 141
Murder, 135

Namaan, 47
Name of God, 132
Nehemias, 33
Noe, 2, 86, 101
Noemi, 20

Obed, 20
Obedience, 5, 22, 134
Original Sin, 2

Paradise, Garden of, 2, 3, 103, 108
Passover, 7, 14, 17, 96

Passover lamb, 14, 53
Patience, 72
Paul, St., 74, 94, 103, 112, 124, 131, 142
Peace, 66
Penance, 97, 98
Pentecost, 15, 17, 78
Peter, St., 46, 49, 60, 64, 93, 109, 110, 111, 123, 132
Pilate, 59
Pillar of fire, 55
Poor and humble, 83
Poverty, 130
Prayer, 120, 121
Preaching, 41
Pride, 140
Priesthood, 10, 11, 101, 102
Prince of Peace, 66
Prodigal son, 69
Promised Land, 16, 18, 45, 63
Prophets, false, 25
Publican, prayer of, 120

Redemption, 3, 28, 43
Red Sea, 43, 48, 91
Remnant in Church, 27
Resurrection, 25, 35, 56, 145. *See also* Lazarus
Resurrection of Jesus, 50, 61, 66, 75, 129, 133, 145
Rock, 57
Ruth, 20

Sabbath Day, 1, 133
Sacrifice, 11, 12
Samson, 19
Samuel, 21
Saul, 21, 22, 141
Second Coming, 77, 126, 150
Sermon on the Mount, 51, 67
Sin, 12, 50, 63, 69, 98, 139
Sinai, 8, 9, 15, 16, 49, 51
Sin of Adam, 2, 3
Sloth, 142
Solomon, 23, 24, 90
Son of David, 65
Son of God, 62, 64, 105, 126, 130, 133
Stephen, St., 114
Suffering Servant, 73

Tabernacle, 9
Tabernacles, feast of, 13, 17
Temple, 23, 24, 29, 31, 54, 67, 90
Temptation, 2, 44
Thomas, St., 61
Tobias, 104
Transfiguration, 9, 49, 62, 150
Trial of Jesus, 59

Unity of the Church, 79
Urias, 135

Virgin-birth, 39, 106
Virginity, 116

Washing of the apostles' feet, 61
Wisdom, 24, 67
Women in the Bible, 117
Word of God, hearing the, 119
Work, 124

Zacchaeus, 137

The reader is referred to Appendix A for further subject headings.